THE RECTOR GIRLS

THE RECTOR GIRLS

GRACE MARIANA RECTOR

NEW DEGREE PRESS

COPYRIGHT © 2021 GRACE MARIANA RECTOR

THE RECTOR GIRLS

ISBN   978-1-63676-935-6   *Paperback*

              978-1-63676-999-8   *Kindle Ebook*

              978-1-63730-103-6   *Ebook*

For my Mama, who loved me unconditionally

CONTENTS

NOTE FROM
THE AUTHOR

———

I drove my mom's car home from the hospital on the night she died. My eyes stayed focused on the road. The streetlights around me blurred as I sped by. I gripped the steering wheel tightly as tears streamed down my face. Suddenly, I realized I had two important things to do: get a tattoo and write a book about my mom's life. My adopted family was in the car, so I shared out loud the two promises I had made my mom years earlier. With tears still in our eyes, we burst into laughter. My mom couldn't leave this world without giving me extremely important tasks, as she often did.

Two years earlier, I told my mom I wanted to get a tattoo. She said, "You better not!" I told her I wanted a tattoo of our family heart, designed by her. She signed every letter she wrote with a heart with six lines around it to show love radiating. Her countenance changed. Then she replied, "That's sweet. But don't get it until I die. I don't wanna see it on you."

On my twenty-first birthday, one week after my mama died, I walked into a tattoo shop. Beside me were four of my "adopted" sisters and my godmother, Margaret. We huddled together. I had no idea what to expect. Only one of us had ever entered a tattoo parlor. I woke up that morning excited, but as I sat in the stiff leather chair, the tattoo needle buzzing, I grew nervous. As the birthday girl, I had no choice but to go first. I looked down at the stencil the tattoo artist had traced. I had taken a picture of my mom's family heart and printed it out. Three of my adopted sisters and my godmother had the same heart tattooed on the inside of their wrists. Although my mom was gone, I had my family—connected by a tattoo of love and solidarity.

Then came my promise to write a book about my mom's life. If you're reading this, I *did it!* One day, she and I were chatting in the backyard. I had an idea I couldn't push aside. I leaned over and asked her, "Mama? Have you ever thought about writing a book? Your life is so different from everyone else."

She looked over at me with a smile and replied, "Actually, yes. Maybe once I retire, I'll write it. I'd name it *Donor, Donor, Donor, Donor.*" She paused and smiled knowingly, "Ya know, for your sperm donor, my two kidney donors, and the financial donor who donated to my office!"

I chuckled at her smart-ass title. "Wow, you've really thought that through haven't you!" I replied. Then I inquired, "Hey Mama, if you don't write the book, can I?"

She smirked and nodded. "Sure! Just don't fuck it up."

. . .

Not only have I written this book to honor my Mama's memory, but also so you could see your own life through a different lens. Many people think a good life is one that goes perfectly according to a preconceived plan. Maybe some people think a perfect life is one that looks like a romantic comedy. But the truth is, we create our own paths. My mom taught me that the positives and negatives of life only impact you as much as you let them. For her, life did not go according to plan, but she didn't give up. She reflected on what she wanted and made it happen. When she hadn't found her life companion by the age of forty-three, but wanted a child, she made it happen. She went to the sperm bank, picked a donor, and got inseminated. She created our small family, which she called "The Rector Girls."

As an only child herself, my mom longed for a bigger family. She looked for opportunities in her life to create that family. The students she mentored as a middle-school counselor became her kids, and eventually, they became my siblings. She baptized me with two godmothers and two godfathers even though most Catholic children only have one of each. She created a big family for me to be a part of. She turned her dreams into reality when life didn't do everything for her.

Living with my mom at our house for eighteen years allowed me to soak up everything she had to offer. One thing I have always admired about her was that she never panicked. As a friend of mine said, "If there were seven buildings on fire around her, she would remain calm. She'd probably even complain about her shoes giving her blisters."

Writing this book gave me a therapeutic space to relive memories with my mom; it made me realize how unique my life is, and it taught me more about my mom through the interviews I conducted with people who knew her. Not only do I hope you learn the lessons she taught me, but I also hope you get to enjoy reading about our adventures. I also bet you will laugh because my Mama never took life too seriously!

Ultimately, the only thing we control is how we react to the events in our lives. My mom taught me to let go and be more present. This skill enables me to focus on my reaction to terrible events that are out of my control.

This book is for individuals who are curious, interested in travel, and want to hear a completely different story. My untraditional family may not seem perfect, but it is perfect for me. This novel is a "creative nonfiction." My mom and I embellish the truth to make our stories more relevant to people we tell stories to, so I hope this story relates to you in some way.

This writing process made me more grateful for all the supportive people I have in my life. While you are reading this book, I hope you take the time to reflect on who the important people in your life are and how they have impacted you. Reflection was key to my mom's life, and it was the reason she decided to become a mother. If you leave this book remembering anything, I hope it is this:

When life doesn't go as planned, take a breath and figure out how you will react to it. If you want better friends, go find them. If you can't stand your blood family, go make your own family. If you don't find your partner when you're twenty-two and cute, surround yourself with incredible friends who support you in every way.

Lastly, I want to thank my "adopted siblings," Arelly, Ale, German, Jorge, Liz, Megan, and Kate, for supporting me through this journey and for laughing with me about stuff mom would say. I also want to thank my godparents, Margaret and Pat, for being my adopted parents; truly, your house is home for me, too.

I couldn't have finished this book without the love and encouragement of my best friend in the world: Rimsha

Nazeer. I love you so much. Thanks also to the people who have kept me sane throughout the worst year of my life: Andria, Patrick, Laura, Nico, Maddie, Matthew, Tommy, and Sania.

Thank you for taking the time to read this story and to immerse yourself in a world full of independent-ass women who talk to strangers, travel across the world, and know when to laugh and when to cry. Welcome to the story of the "Rector Girls."

All my love,
Grace Mariana Rector

BEFORE

CHAPTER 1

CHOOSE YOUR COMMUNITY

———

My mom brought freshly baked cranberry oatmeal cookies to the dining room and rearranged all the sperm donor applications on the table to make room for the snacks. She needed her friends well-fed if they were to help her pick my future biological father. Her former coworker, Adela, raised one bio sheet and said, "Ooh! I like this one. He's in medical school *aaaaand* he says that he 'loves his mother.'" She smiled softly and clung tightly to the donor bio as if it were a golden ticket.

Another old coworker and friend, Kathy, jumped into the conversation, "Wait, is that sperm donor #1954? He has a history of medical issues in his family, so I don't think he's a good pick." Kathy wrote on her notepad intently. She had dual columns for pros and cons for each potential sperm donor. Her train of thought was interrupted by my mom's best friend, Margaret, who met my mom when she was in college.

She exclaimed, "What about donor #9931? He has a Master's in Education, which means he is smart, and he likes to travel. If you had a baby with this guy, your kid would definitely have the travel bug like you." Kathy added donor #9931 to her list and wrote "travel" and "education" under the pros column.

My mom, Pam Rector, passed more cookies to her girl-friends, known as the "Cookie Exchange Girls." They had first become friends when working together in an elementary school twenty years earlier. Every year, they met to exchange cookies at Adela's house during the week before Christmas. They could always tell it was a cookie exchange when Adela laid out her white, green, and red hand-embroidered Christmas tablecloth on the table. Adela strictly reminded her friends to keep the tablecloth clean because she did not have time to clean it again before Christmas.

While cookies were the main event, each woman would bring some food to the potluck. Before they ate, they would exchange gifts, sometimes an ornament or souvenirs from their travels. But this year, my mom handed out donor bio sketches instead. Together, the ladies reviewed the bios of potential sperm donors for my mom's hypothetical child. The long, wooden dining room table was obscured by hundreds of pieces of paper and plates with an assortment of cookies. My mom leaned over to another friend she used to work with, Jo Ann, to grab a chocolate peanut butter cookie. She placed it in her mouth with her left hand and reached for another donor bio with her right. The women sat around the table munching on six different cookies while reading over donor descriptions. The cookies included ginger crinkles, almond krunze, sugar cookies, cranberry white chocolate oatmeal, chocolate peanut butter, and Mexican wedding cake. Each woman read quietly until a donor description stood out, then loudly declared her discovery to the group. It was like picking out a dress to the prom, except the stakes were much higher.

When Pam turned forty years old, she decided she wanted to become a mother. Just one problem. She didn't have a partner. She knew she could wait and wait, hoping for the right guy to come along and raise a child with her. But, as she told a good friend of hers, "If I don't do it now, my juicy bits will dry up!" No one grows up wanting to be a single mom, and neither did my mom, but she knew she wanted to be a mother. She couldn't let a man inhibit her goal. Before committing to becoming a mom, she had to discern whether it was the right path for her. My mom reflected at a Catholic silent retreat. After hours of silence and sitting alone with her thoughts, she confirmed her desire to become my mother. She turned to her girlfriends to help her on this new journey.

It seems simple enough to read through bios and pick the biological father of your child, but my mom couldn't pick just any guy. My Mama dated Latino men throughout her life, so she wanted a Latino sperm donor. However, her parents told her, "You get to pick who the father is, so choose a white man. We want a grandchild who looks like us." They held a traditional and conservative view. They didn't want a Latino sperm donor because they wanted me to match my ethnically Irish and British grandparents. Although she still wanted a Latino sperm donor, my mom understood that it may be better to have a child who looks more similar to her so that her child would be identifiable as her kid, especially as a single mom.

My mom drew a star on donor #7382's application and asked, after reading it a few times, "What do you think of this one?" She asked Margaret, who was in the middle of analyzing the bio on her lap. Margaret not only had stars on hers, but she had highlighted important traits and written notes in the margins. Margaret gently took the document that my mom held in front of her and began to calmly read the donor's traits. While Margaret read, Kathy tapped my mom's shoulder and excitedly said, "This one has good handwriting! He must be smart, or organized!"

Sil, another friend of my mom's, passed a document to my mom and said, "This one is tall and skinny. He's also Italian, so your child won't burn as easily as you do, Pam!" The Cookie Exchange Girls roared in laughter as they each imagined what my mom's baby would look like. After reading through many donor bios, the group discussed the candidates and agreed on the same top two donors. Following the meeting, my mom went to a sperm donor bank to purchase the taped interviews with each of her top candidates. Then Jo Ann brought a cassette player from her work to my mom's house so they could listen to the candidate interviews.

The tape began with a crackle and a pause. Then they heard the chuckle of donor #5102. The tape rolled as each of my mom's friends took notes in their own way. Margaret scribbled her notes on a piece of paper, Adela closed her eyes and paid attention to the details, and Kathy observed my mom's reactions.

The recording ended. It was decision time. "Thoughts?" Margaret asked my mom. Pam paused and reflected before speaking. "He seemed really social, and natural in the conversation… I like that he cracked jokes even in a sperm donor interview." Margaret added, "Yes! And you could tell by the tone of the interviewer's voice that she liked him. He seems charismatic." Kathy nodded while she chewed on one of Sil's cinnamon sugar cookies.

After listening to the tape of the second donor, they continued their analysis. Then Kathy asked, "So which one is it?" My mom gently smiled and said, "donor 5102." All her friends nodded in agreement. My Mama's eyes watered with joy. Margaret placed her hand over my mom's.

"Fuck!" my mom exclaimed, "Well, that's over." She chuckled to her girlfriends. "Now I just need to go get inseminated. Woo!"

But I'm getting ahead of myself. Literally.

Although they chose donor 5102, my mom still had to get inseminated and cross her fingers that it worked. My mom purchased several vials of donor 5102's sperm. Maybe she'd get pregnant on the first try; maybe she wouldn't; maybe she'd want two children instead of one. The first insemination was unsuccessful. But my mom didn't give up. She got inseminated a second time, and one of millions of sperm fought its way past the others to fertilize one of my Mama's eggs.

On February 22, 1999, as the sun was rising at 6:22 a.m., my mom's life changed. I was born. Although a single mother, my mom didn't birth me alone. Margaret, my godmother, and Mark, my godfather, accompanied my mom in the delivery room. Most women in labor hold one person's hand, but my mom held two.

. . .

As I grew up, my Mama and I got to know each other more and more. She was my first friend, my first enemy, my first everything. "Mama" was also the first word I uttered, despite my grandpa's attempts to make me say his name first. She and I would lay on the carpet and just talk. We'd cuddle on the couch, or as we called it, "snuggle buggle," while watching TV. She held me in her arms when I couldn't stop crying. We baked the famous Rector Girl brownies. She traveled across the world for work and took me with her. I had no idea about all the adventures we would go on over the next twenty years.

CHAPTER 2

ASK AND YOU SHALL RECEIVE

After my fourth birthday, my mom took me to El Salvador for a work trip. She was the director of the Center for Service and Action at Loyola Marymount University (LMU) in Los Angeles. Once a year, she took a group of students to another country for a service-learning experience. This was the first time she took me with her. In addition to handling fifteen college students for this trip, she also had to handle a toddler.

Mom packed bags for two, plus all the crap a toddler needs. Once at the airport, she calmly put me in the stroller, despite all the chaos around her. After strapping me in, my Mama pushed the stroller with her left hand and carried the two suitcases with her right hand. She pushed and pulled as best as she could, even stopping from time to time when a suitcase would fall. If that wasn't enough, I started crying. Not one of those little cries, but rather one of those tired, ear-piercing shrieks. She had to choose her battles and this one wasn't worth it, so she trekked on to the check-in desk and checked our bags. Finally! She now only had to juggle me, my stroller, and her backpack.

Being a single mom is hard work, but she pulled it off. Travel was important to her, so she would do whatever it took to keep traveling, even with a loud, screeching toddler. I watched her in awe as she managed one hundred things at once and still stayed calm. Instead of leaving me at home, every time my mom had a work trip coming up, I knew I'd get to accompany her across the globe.

A couple days after we arrived in El Salvador, my mom enrolled me in a local preschool for a few weeks while she worked. I remember the nervous energy I carried in my little stomach as I walked into a new school without my mom. Oh, I also didn't speak Spanish.

I sat on the colorful rainbow carpet dragging my fingers along familiar shapes. I looked around the classroom. It was smaller than my preschool in Los Angeles, but the white board and the bright flyers on the walls were familiar. I'd seen similar weather signs in my classroom in the United States.

My exploring eyes stopped at the teacher. Señora Sandra towered over me. She wore a long green dress, the color of moss, and a mean look on her face. She had a ruler in her hand that she wielded like a sword. She pointed to a colorful sign with pictures of clouds, rain, and the sun that was divided into seven pieces. Every time she hit a word at the top, all the kids responded, except me. She glared at me, and I looked back with empty eyes. *What was I supposed to be doing?* I didn't know if I should mimic the sounds I was hearing or if I should give up and cry. The teacher looked at me and said, "MI - ER - CO - LES." She looked at me expectantly and I sounded back, "ME - AIR - KO - LE." She softened her eyes. "*Bien*," she said, and picked another child. I think I got it right because she didn't yell at me, but I had no idea what the word meant. When other kids became restless and looked less bored, I knew it was free time. The other kids got up one by one, scattering to different parts of the room. They knew what to do.

I was lost.

I hopped up from the rug and ran to the nearest group of students huddled together. I leaned in and stood on my tiptoes to see what they were looking at. *Dress up!* The kids rummaged through a box of costumes and created their characters piece by piece. *Finally! Something I knew how to do.* I couldn't contain my joy and grabbed the fluffiest purple skirt I'd ever seen. I yelled, "Can I be a princess?"

They paused and looked at one another. One brunette girl with golden skin said, "*¿Qué dijó? ¿Quiere ser una princesa?*"

Her friend, who was dressed in a yellow T-shirt and green shorts, shrugged and nodded her head. I took that as a yes to being a princess and proceeded to dance around with my new friends.

. . .

After a long first day, my mom picked me up from school. She scooped me up and asked me about my day. I excitedly told her, "Mama! It was fun. I wore a dress. I have friends. The teacher is scary. I don't know what they said. It was fun." I cuddled into her, happy to have someone who understood the words coming out of my mouth.

"Good job, Gracie," my mom told me as she put me back on the ground, "I know it may have been hard not knowing what they said. You were patient and will learn more and more words in Spanish every day." During this trip, and every other trip after, my mom never coddled me. She constantly threw me into new environments so I would learn to adapt and relate to people different from me.

Later that week, my mom took me to a gathering in the backyard of a Salvadoran woman she worked with. I leaned over to my mom and tugged her hand, "Hey Mama—what are they cooking?" I pointed to three Salvadoran women standing behind a grill. Each woman moved dough between her hands like magic.

"Why don't we go ask them?" my mom replied. She walked me over to the señoras. My mom kindly asked the women if they'd teach me how to make *pupusas*, a national Salvadoran dish, and they replied unanimously, *"Sí! Claro!"* I stayed with these women for the whole night, helping them make balls of dough stuffed with beans and cheese. I felt independent and grown up, although I knew my mom was somewhere watching me the whole time.

. . .

While this trip was my first, it was far from the last adventure I went on with my mom. She brought me on work trips, and we went on vacations to different countries around the world. She taught me the importance of immersing myself in new cultures and learning new languages. My mom and I traveled internationally together for her work or just to expose ourselves to a different culture. We were each other's travel buddy, each other's entertainment on long plane rides, and each other's caretaker if one of us got sick. My mom took time at the end of each day to ask me, "What did you learn? What did you see? Who did you meet?" She wanted me to practice my reflection skills, even in my toddler years. A year after our trip to El Salvador, my mom brought me to San Lucas Toliman in Guatemala for another work trip.

One day, I stood by my mom's side as she talked to adults about boring things. I grew restless and looked around me. I saw an old-looking church to my left, and to my right I saw a cloud of dust. I squinted my eyes, intrigued by the action, and saw five girls running in circles in the dirt. They laughed and played. I saw one girl tap another and then run away. *They're playing tag!* I turned my focus away from the adults and onto the kids. My curiosity gained the best of me and I tugged on my mom's pants, "Mama? Can I go play with them?" I asked, while pointing to the group of girls running around. She nodded and I leaped up with joy, then ran to the kids. I still didn't speak much Spanish, so I just smiled. They all stopped running for a moment and stared. They looked at my crocs and my jeans and my T-shirt and my face. They took me in bit by bit. I was terrified. I wasn't sure what to think. Then one girl relaxed her face and stepped toward me. She leaned forward and tagged me on the shoulder then ran away. *I was "it!" I knew how to play!*

Among the group was an eight-year-old girl named Lesbia. She and I stayed close together throughout the game. I did not understand the words she said, but the constant smile on her face and her eagerness to help me in the game indicated to me she wanted to be friends.

On another day, my mom and I stopped by the shop that Lesbia's parents owned. "Buenas tardes, Señora." My mom began. *¿Quería preguntar si tu hija puede salir a jugar con la mía por una hora?* "I wanted to ask if your daughter can play with mine for an hour?" My mom spoke fluent Spanish. Her mom agreed, and I excitedly took Lesbia's hand. I ran with her to the church cafeteria where the student volunteers from my mom's work ate their meals. I went to the fridge and grabbed a Fanta soda for my friend. Then an old white man urgently came toward us. "She is not allowed in here!" he yelled, "You cannot bring people in here! This is just for volunteers!" I tightly clenched the bottle, grabbed Lesbia's hand, and we ran out and sat on the street. I gave her the soda and we sat there in stunned silence.

Later when I saw my mom, I ran to give her a hug. She leaned over and hugged me tightly. "What's wrong, Girlie? What happened?"

"I . . . I . . ." I teared up, "I was trying to be nice . . . and get a soda for my friend . . . but then someone at the church yelled at me and told me I couldn't bring other people in." She held me a bit longer, not saying anything.

Then she said, "Sometimes people are unkind to certain people because they have judgments about them before they even know them. You didn't do anything wrong, Girlie. The man who yelled at you probably didn't want Lesbia coming in because he wants to keep it just for American students. That is not right, but it's a rule he is following."

Something I appreciated about my mom was how she always spoke to me like an adult. Even when I was five years old, she treated me like her counterpart who was capable of handling serious topics. She treated me like an adult from the beginning because she needed a companion and also so I could understand reality. She knew how harsh the world is and hoped that by exposing me to it, I would be less surprised when things went wrong.

She never lied to me. Even when I asked her if the tooth fairy was real, she said, "What do you think?" At age five, I lost my first tooth. I bit into my apple and a white seed fell out—a seed that turned out to be my tooth. All the kids at preschool were excited and jealous of me because losing a tooth meant the tooth fairy would visit and leave money under my pillow. I got home and showed my Mama the gaping hole where my tooth had been. I was so proud. I could hardly fall asleep that night because I was so excited to receive money for my tooth!

In the morning, I yawned loudly, rubbed the sleep out of my eyes, and looked under my pillow. Nothing. I threw my pillow on the floor and pulled back the sheets. Nothing. The tooth was there, but there was no money. So naturally, I walked to my mom's room and woke her up. "Mama—you forgot to put money under my pillow."

I don't know if I missed out on anything by not believing in fairy tales and mythical creatures, but I'm grateful she raised me the way she did. She never told me Santa Claus or the Easter Bunny didn't exist; she would just answer me with honesty. When I was four, I saw a Santa Claus in a mall. I noticed he was wearing red Converse shoes. I said, "Mama, he has the same shoes as German. Is he German?" I compared Santa Claus to my twenty-three-year-old "adopted" brother. My mom just told me, "Yep! He has the same shoes as German. It's not German, but it's a different guy." Her response confirmed this was not Santa and all Santas at malls were just young men dressing up.

As I grew older, she trusted me more and more. She enabled my fast-paced maturity by exposing me to the harsh realities of the world. When I was in eighth grade, my mom took me on another service-learning trip to Kigali, Rwanda. Rwanda is a beautiful country with a complex and dark history of genocide—something most kids don't learn about. Nonetheless, she knew I could handle it, and she prepared me. We attended interviews with survivors of the genocide to learn about the history and what the government did to promote reconciliation between ethnic groups. My mom explained to me, "These interviews are going to be sad, but we need to be grateful to the person sharing for having the courage to tell her story. Be respectful." We listened to interview after interview and my heart tightened. One woman shared that after her mother, father, and brothers were killed, she barely escaped and hid in a bathroom for five days waiting for the perpetrators of the genocide to move on. It was a lot to take in, but I was so grateful my mom trusted me to be mature. She brought me with her so I could learn about the world outside of Los Angeles and the critical inquiry skills needed for complex topics like the Rwandan genocide. We'd reflect at the end of the night on our emotions and about the things we learned. If she had not pushed me to think deeply about these experiences, I might not have understood the full impact of the program.

. . .

While we went on many trips for her work, we also went on fun mother-daughter trips to Italy, Peru, Cuba, Nicaragua, Puerto Rico, India, and so many more. When I was twelve years old, we spent three weeks traveling around Italy. I remember being in Florence and at 10:00 a.m., my mom leaned over to me and said, "Should we get gelato for breakfast? Should we do it?"

I excitedly responded, "Yes!" That day, we ate four different gelatos. We walked the cobblestone streets taking pictures and talking, and then we stopped at a restaurant that was packed with people. My mom told me, "Always go to the full restaurants. They're there for a reason."

My mom was my favorite person to be with. She was fun! She was loving! She was adventurous! She was the perfect travel buddy. In Italy, we stayed in a little house with a patio. After settling into the place, we decided to go on an adventure. We went to a huge shop that sold focaccia bread and bought ten different types. Surrounded by half eaten loaves, we sat on the patio playing cards. We laughed and the sun shone down on us, keeping the bread toasty.

Later that day, we went to the beach and while my Mama sat under her umbrella reading a book, I laid on the sand, thinking. I loved traveling with my mom but sometimes I wished there was someone to play with, like a kid my age who I could run around with or swim with. I laid on the towel feeling restless until I saw three kids in the ocean passing a volleyball. My eyes lit up.

"Mama, look at them playing volleyball. It looks so fun." I said.

"You should go play with them then," she offered.

I paused, "Uh . . . I don't know. I don't know them. I don't want to be weird."

"What's the worst that they say? No? . . . come on, just go say, 'Can I play with you guys?' and see what happens."

My Mama encouraged me again to ask for what I want because the only way you will get it is by asking. "Ask and you shall receive" is what she used to tell me.

I took a few minutes to build up enough courage. Then I got off my towel and trudged into the water, heading straight for a group of kids I didn't know. My heart pounded. I was so scared of getting rejected. The two boys and the girl noticed me coming their way. I waved a little too soon and awkwardly walked closer until they could hear me.

"Uh . . . hi. Can I... play with you guys?" I gestured to the volleyball, pointed to myself, and then at them. "Por favor," I added, which was Spanish, not Italian, but I think they got my intention.

Then the tall boy in the middle stepped forward and said, "*¿Hablas español?*" and my face lit up.

"¡Sí! ¡Sí! Hablo español!" I replied in my slightly American accent. He laughed and replied in Spanish, "You can play with us." I sighed in relief and a huge smile replaced my nervous tight lips. I looked at my mom on the shore and smiled. I flashed her two thumbs up!

I played volleyball with these kids for two long hours. It was an unforgettable part of my trip. My mom gave me the courage to go out of my comfort zone, and it was worth it.

As I grew up, we traveled more, we got busier, but she supported me through everything I did. She was my biggest cheerleader and also my biggest critic. She would come to my performances and afterward she would hug me and say, "You were amazing! I love you! But I heard you go flat on one of the notes." It was contradictory feedback, but I appreciated it, nonetheless. While she could be harsh, she celebrated everything. And I mean *everything*. When a guy liked me back for the first time, she established it as my first "crush back" and took me to a store to buy me a bottle of nail polish to celebrate.

Soon I graduated middle school and was onto high school. I went to an all-girls Catholic high school, and she was so excited. My Mama was a very spiritual and Catholic person. She prayed to God often and always wore a cross around her neck. One of her biggest values was education, so although the tuition at my high school cost a pretty penny, she thought it was worth it.

. . .

During the spring break of my senior year of high school, my mom and I vacationed in Puerto Rico and got to enjoy the sunny beach. I was eighteen, so I could enjoy a couple drinks with her. We approached the bar and I felt for my wallet in my pocket with an excited hand; I couldn't wait to show my ID to the bartender because I could legally buy a drink. The bartender handed me a colorful raspberry mojito. My mom rarely drank, but that night we both enjoyed drinks in a little bar in the city. We sat outside on cheap wire chairs, but we didn't notice how uncomfortable they were because we were having such a good time. My mom is a workaholic, so I loved being with her on vacation away from Wi-Fi.

She leaned across the table, reminiscing, "I was a sophomore in high school, and I desperately wanted to play a sport, but women weren't allowed at the time, so I was the 'water girl' for the soccer team. I loved watching the boys play from the sidelines, a front row seat. Just like you, I was always friends with more guys than girls. There wasn't any drama, and we would just hang out. Then I dated the captain of the soccer team—a British guy!"

I was shocked; she never talked about guys from her past, let alone stories from high school. I was so happy to be on the receiving end of her storytelling. We continued the exchange of stories for the rest of the vacation. The next day, we laid on the beach; well, she laid in a chair under the umbrella as I laid under the sun. After all, the sperm donor my mom and her girlfriends had chosen was Italian; thus, I could tan very well, whereas my mom had sensitive, pale skin that would turn red after thirty seconds under the sun. We laid there next to each other with only shade separating us—laughing, chatting, and reading our books. Later, I convinced her to come into the ocean for just a couple minutes. I was so happy, and she was too. We forgot about everything else—work, school, responsibilities—and just enjoyed one another's presence.

But this feeling of carefree happiness didn't last long.

CHAPTER 3

BE AN INDEPENDENT-ASS WOMAN

———

My Mama and I made our way home from Puerto Rico to Los Angeles, where my "adopted" sister, Arelly, pulled up to the curb at the airport. Her head popped out of the car. I excitedly ran over to greet her. She doesn't like hugs, but she lets me hug her because she knows how affectionate I am. After letting her go, I picked up our bags and tossed them into the trunk.

On the five-minute drive home from the airport, my Mama was very quiet. Arelly asked Mom, "How was the trip?"

My mom looked back at her with wandering eyes. I sat in the back seat hearing my mom reply, "Uh . . . it . . . was . . ."

She paused. "I . . . ." I leaned forward to see my mom sitting there with blank eyes and blinking frequently.

Arelly looked back at her with furrowed eyebrows. "Are you okay, Mom?" Arelly asked with a concerned voice. My mom didn't respond for a long time. Then she took a breath,

"I'm fine. I'm just tired." At first, I wasn't concerned. But seeing her struggle to talk was frightening. She never had difficulty getting words out.

By the time we got home, she was still incoherent. I said gently, "Mama, you don't seem okay, are you sure?"

She rolled her eyes. "I'm fine. Just let me lie down for fifteen minutes." She walked by Arelly and me and into her bedroom and closed the door. We stood outside of mom's room and looked each other in the eyes. The shape of Arelly's face blurred with my tears. My lip quivered. Arelly looked away so she wouldn't cry. Tears fell down my face. *What is wrong with my Mama? Is she okay? Is she sick? Is it worse? Something isn't right.*

Arelly called my "adopted" brother, German. She explained what was happening and I could hear him say through the phone, "Mom needs to call the doctor right now!"

I opened the door to my mom's room. I neared her bed. I couldn't hold back my little sobs. She turned over to face me and said, "Grace! I . . . said . . . I . . . I . . . am fine . . . tired . . . I'm just . . . tired." Her tone and incoherence scared me. I lost control of my wavering voice. I cried, "Mama! Something is not right, please call the doctor, or a nurse or something . . . please. Mama." I crawled into bed with her as she called the nurse on her phone.

I told the nurse about my mom's loss for words. The nurse responded, "She is experiencing symptoms of a stroke, you need to hang up and call 911."

I began sobbing and grabbed my phone against my mom's pleas that it wasn't that serious.

"This is 911. What's your emergency?"

"I'm calling because my mom isn't able to form coherent sentences and may have experienced a stroke. Please come quickly."

I don't remember what happened next. The 911 responders asked me questions and I mindlessly replied. I hung up and stared at my phone. *I just called 911.* My heart raced. Tears were still running down my face. I just sat there next to my mom, frozen. "Grace," my mom said. "Grace!" she said more loudly to break my frozen countenance. "Go start packing a bag. I need reading glasses, extra underwear, a bathrobe, toothbrush, toothpaste, and concealer!" She'd been to the hospital so many times before that she knew exactly what she needed. I rushed around her bathroom gathering her supplies. I reached for her concealer with a shaky hand. I gripped it tightly, but my hand kept shaking so violently that I dropped it.

The sound of sirens was faint at first. The sirens you hear every once in a while. By the time the sound could pierce my ears, I realized the ambulance was coming for my mom. My mom shifted in bed attempting to get up. "Mama! Wait. They'll come and get you."

She shrugged off my comment and proceeded to get up. She looked at me with frustration, "Let me fucking walk." She paused and looked at me. My mom was strong willed and did not like to be pitied. In a gentler tone, she assured me, "I'm fine." She stood up with me by her side and walked straight out of her room, down the hall, to the front door, across the lawn, and laid herself down on the stretcher.

I sat next to her in the ambulance, terrified out of my mind. She laid there, cracking jokes as they took her vitals. She took her phone with her wherever she went, and the ambulance was no exception. She typed an email with total focus as if she weren't lying on a stretcher. "Excuse me, ma'am," a paramedic tried to interrupt her concentration.

She looked up and he continued, "We need you to put your phone down so we can conduct some tests." She nodded and continued texting. She replied as she typed, "Let me just finish this email, then I'll be done." She took her time with the message while the paramedics kept a surprised look on their faces. I finally heard the "woosh" notification of an email being sent, and she handed me the phone. The paramedics proceeded with the tests in the ambulance.

We went through a set of double doors in the emergency room. My mom casually laid on the stretcher, and I nervously followed behind. A doctor approached us. He introduced himself, then began routine tests for signs of a stroke. "If you could raise both arms please," he asked. My Mama raised both arms, and the strength in both arms was equal. "Good," the doctor announced, "Now can you smile for me?" He wanted to make sure neither side was drooping—a clear sign of a stroke. My mom smiled with only one side raised and, for a split second, I lost my breath. Then she broke into a full smile and said, "Just kidding!" I exhaled and wasn't sure whether to laugh or cry.

My mom always taught me to be independent and strong despite the challenges that faced me. The doctor continued his exam and informed us she had suffered a transient ischemic attack (TIA), or a mini stroke with no evident permanent damage. However, this episode gave me the same fear and anxiety I had experienced when she underwent a kidney transplant a few years earlier.

At seven years old, death was an abstract idea that I didn't fully understand. When she planned to have the kidney transplant, I began shopping for moms. I was young and didn't know what a surgery entailed, so I believed she would die. A few days before the surgery, I laid next to my mom in bed. I leaned over and said, "Mama, I was thinking I could live with Donna if you die." I cuddled into her arms and she replied, "Huh?" I continued to process, ". . . but if I lived with Donna, she would have to take care of two kids. Hmmm. That's not a good idea . . . what about Gina? My friend's mom at school loves me. She could be my mom." My mom held me close, and a tear fell down her cheek. I laid in her arms, a few days before her major surgery, sharing my logical choices for replacement mothers. My Mama always taught me to be honest, no matter how harsh. So, I told her I feared she would die.

Eleven years later, at eighteen, I was still terrified. As a child, I had heard of the concept of death but didn't know how it could impact me. As a young adult, I understood the reality of death and knew I could not lose my mom without falling apart. My mom is part of me and losing her would be so damaging. Her health scare shocked me and deepened my awareness of her impermanence. I didn't know what I'd do if I lost her.

CHAPTER 4

TRAVEL WHENEVER POSSIBLE

—

As a senior in high school, I prepared for a new chapter in my life: college. I was excited to attend Georgetown University in Washington, DC, but I hated to think of leaving my mom alone. I became aware of the fragility of life. Who knows what could happen to my mom if I were away? I had to trust that my extended family would take care of her in my absence. Although my mom is my only family member by blood, my chosen family means everything to me. Considering I am an only child, and my mom is an only child, I had quite the entourage at my graduation. The members of my chosen family who attended included two godmothers, one of my three godfathers, three of my "adopted" siblings, and one of my god-sisters. I am grateful to my mom for creating our family.

. . .

About twenty-five years earlier, my mom added four important people to our family. She worked as a counselor at Lennox Middle School (LMS) once upon a time. I've only heard these stories through other people, but I can imagine how fun and wonderful she must have been in her twenties and thirties. As a counselor at LMS, she learned Spanish, grew close with the knucklehead kids, and created educational programs that continue to this day. The majority of students were from low-income Latino families, and often had complicated family situations. This made my mom's role as a guidance counselor even more pertinent.

As she worked with students who were struggling in school, participating in gangs, or dealing with issues at home, she realized most of the students didn't have mentors or someone looking out for them. Many students often took care of their younger siblings and didn't have the support to pursue goals beyond high school or even middle school. In response to these issues, my Mama created the "Adopt a Student" program at LMS. The program encouraged teachers and staff to sign up and "adopt" or mentor a student. The goal was to provide students with role models and advocates that they didn't have previously. Naturally, my mom went above and beyond, and "adopted" four students: Arelly, Alejandra, German, and Jorge.

. . .

In 1992, Arelly was eleven years old. My mom had known her since she was in kindergarten. She was a smart kid and took notes intensely. She had different colored highlighters and kept her notes color coded. She wore black skinny jeans and a black Depeche Mode T-shirt. She wore a black choker and black sneakers. She was sitting in third-period class when a teacher's assistant rushed into the room and announced, "I have a note for Arelly Saldaña." Arelly looked up from her notes and raised her hand to identify herself. The class TA walked over to her and dropped the note on her desk. She took the white notecard and read to herself:

"Hi Arelly!
I would love to adopt you to my family.
From,
Ms. Rector"

Though Arelly often hid her emotions, she couldn't hide her smile. She was so excited that Ms. Rector had picked her to be one of her adopted students. She felt seen. It meant so much to her that my mom chose to adopt her out of all the students at LMS.

Another one of my mom's adopted children was Ale. She knew my mom, Ms. Rector, as the school counselor who helped her sister graduate from middle school. In sixth grade, Ale's teacher asked each student to write a thank-you letter to someone who positively impacted their lives, and Ale chose mom. She wrote to Ms. Rector:

"Thank you for your help with my sister. She would not have graduated without your support. Me and my family are so thankful."

My mom subsequently invited Ale to her office and asked her, "Would you be interested in coming to the Mentorship Picnic? I started a program for students to find mentors and I'd like you to come meet my adopted students." Ale followed my mom to the outdoor picnic and sat down at a table next to three strangers: Arelly, German, and Jorge. These three strangers became her adopted siblings.

My mom took all four adopted students out to dinner for their birthdays, took them on vacations, and invited them over to her house for Christmas. Every summer while the students were in high school, my mom took them on different trips. They visited San Diego, Lake Tahoe, and San Francisco. At first, they called her "Ms. Rector" because she was their guidance counselor; however, as they continued into high school and maintained their bond with her, they began to call her "Mom." Ale was the first to call her "Mom" and Arelly was the last.

Flash forward to 1999 when my mom's adopted students were eighteen and nineteen years old, their little sister, Grace, was born; that's me. My mom introduced them to me as the "Big Kids," since they are my mom's kids, but older than me. The four of them are a big part of my life. They show up for every life event.

. . .

Graduation was a big deal because it represented the end of my time living at home with my mom. She raised me to love travel and exploration, so we both knew once I left for college, I'd only be back for the holidays. It was a joyful celebration but also a little sad because I wouldn't be with my mom every day. Before our bittersweet finale, my mom and I talked about my goals and plans. I hesitated to express my desire to travel because her health was so uncertain. She had just had a mini stroke two months earlier. I still wanted to travel with the same level of enthusiasm as my mom had instilled in me, but I was more cautious. She noticed, and told me her famous line, "Gracie girl, I'm fine!" She continued, "Go travel! The Big Kids are here to take care of me."

With my mom's words ringing in my ear, I got on the plane headed for an Eastern European trip with my best friend from high school, Julia. Although it was my first backpacking trip without my mom, her advice followed me everywhere I went. From the way I packed my carry-on bag, to the way I organized my travel documents, she guided me. One tip she gave me was to put essential items in your carry on, including medicine, toiletries, and a change of clothes just in case your checked bag got lost.

Usually this packing tip wouldn't matter, but this time it did. We waited around the baggage claim carousel for two hours in Vienna, Austria. We waited and waited while everyone around us found their bags and went on their way. After waiting for two hours a man approached us and asked, "Can't find your bags?" We shook our heads. "Right this way." He led us to the customer service desk.

The airline had lost our bags. We had no idea when we'd get them back. For a moment, I angrily gripped the straps of my backpack until my nails hit my palms. I stopped. I inhaled and exhaled. I took another deep breath and thought of what my mom would say, "Don't panic. You'll be fine without extra clothes for a couple of days." I had packed my medicine, hygiene, and extra underwear in my carry-on, so I was fine. The next morning, I woke up and put on the same outfit. Rather than grump about my clothes not smelling the freshest, I just laughed and said to Julia, "Do you like my outfit today?" She smirked. I tried to embody my mom's ability to find humor in everything. Two days later, we finally got our clothes back (in Krakow, Poland) and I was very happy to put on a new outfit.

Julia and I traveled around Austria, Czech Republic, Poland, Slovakia, and Hungary for three weeks. We visited museums, went on tours, tried local foods, white-water rafted in Poland, biked through the Slovakian forests, took an evening cruise down the Danube river in Budapest, found a silent disco in a warehouse in the Czech Republic, and even crashed a French embassy party. As a traveler, I take risks. That is definitely something my mom taught me.

We were looking closely at the John Lennon wall art in Prague when we noticed some live music and chatter behind us. There was a large yellow building with towering iron gates and a velvet rope in front with a guard watching it. I saw crowds of people beyond the gates walking around to different booths; it looked like a fair. I saw a few people exit the gates with wide smiles on their faces.

I turned to Julia and said, "What do you think that is?"

She replied with a confused look, "I have no idea."

I wonder who is allowed to attend, I thought. I looked back at Julia with a daring look and walked up to the guard. "Hello! What is this event?" I inquired.

"It's a fair for the French embassy," he replied curtly.

"Are we able to attend?" I said in as confident a tone as I could muster.

He looked back at me sternly and I thought there was no chance we'd be able to enter. He cleared his throat, "Yes—the entrance and security are that way," he said pointing to the building entrance.

We thanked him and walked away calmly. Then I looked at Julia and excitedly yelled, "OMG! We get to go to the embassy!" She laughed at my enthusiasm and followed my lead.

Sure enough, we got through security, showed our passports, and entered the event to witness live music and check out the little booths. There was one booth with hundreds of colorful macarons, and I couldn't help but purchase two. It was a beautiful event. I silently thanked my mom for giving me the confidence to ask for what I want. She helped Julia and me discover this hidden beauty. My mom had been to Budapest years earlier, and thus, she sent me a list of places to visit during our trip.

After my trip with Julia, I flew from Budapest to Florence to meet up with two of the Big Kids: German and Arelly. I was overcome with joy when they stepped out of their hotel to greet me. I ran up to Arelly and almost knocked her over with my hug. I'd never traveled with the Big Kids without my mom, so this was a new adventure. We walked around Florence on the cobblestone streets. Then we waited in line to see *the David*. Later, we searched the city for the focaccia shop my mom and I had gone to eight years earlier. We had no luck, but the memory of that shop still lingers in my mind.

On our first night, we went out to dinner at a classic Italian restaurant. I sat next to German and across from Arelly. We glanced over the menus.

I asked, "What do we wanna get?"

Arelly, appearing aloof, suggested, "The shrimp pasta looks yummy."

I said, "Ooh, I want to get the Caprese salad!"

German replied, "Ugh! Is it with buffalo mozzarella? I can't eat that." He paused, "But get it anyway!" I nodded and smiled slightly at Arelly. We always tease German for complaining, but siblings are siblings. I changed the subject.

"Hey," I said, grabbing Arelly's attention. "Look what he just posted." I pointed my phone at her to show her a picture of a guy I had a crush on. He was at the beach during sunset with his arm around a beautiful brunette girl wearing a loose white dress.

"OMG! Who is she?" Arelly pointed to the girl standing too close to him to "just" be a friend.

I shrugged. "I don't know . . . probably some girl from his school . . . damn," I said with a disappointed glance.

German interrupted, "Who?"

Arelly and I always got into trouble with Mom and the Big Kids for being too cliquey. Throughout high school, Arelly and I went out to a movie and dinner every month, making us super close. Often when we went out to dinner with Mom and the other Big Kids, Arelly and I would spend thirty minutes taking pictures in the bathroom together. I apologized to German and explained what I was talking about.

The waiter interrupted my chatter. "Good evening! How are you all doing tonight?" he asked.

"We're good. Long day of walking around the city. We're only here for a few days," I babbled.

He commented, "Ahh, so a quick vacation to Florence?"

"Yes! We're on a sibling trip around Europe." I declared.

One can see that German, Arelly, and I are not related by blood, but we truly act like siblings. Sometimes we love each other and sometimes we can't stand each other. Germ and Arelly were thirty-six at the time, and I was eighteen.

The waiter left for the kitchen and returned with free red wine. I drooled in excitement. I reached for the glass with so much enthusiasm I knocked it over, right onto my white shirt. I looked down and saw the stain stick out from the white fabric like blood. I glanced up at Germ and Arelly and we all busted out laughing. The three of us laughed so hard at my clumsy self, but also because mom was always the one who spilled food and drinks on herself. I guess I inherited her clumsiness, too. That's why my mom always wore patterned dresses; if she spilled on her dress, the pattern would hide the stain. The patterned dresses she wore were always so complex and colorful. She created a complex and colorful life for me filled with extended family, that allowed me to sit there with my brother and sister, halfway across the world.

The next day, German, Arelly, and I flew to Barcelona, Spain. The first thing we did upon arrival was go out for some paella and sangria. I placed a spoonful of the delicious rice in my mouth and closed my eyes. The soft rice blended with the subtle crunch of the grilled vegetables. My mouth watered from the mix of rich flavors. I opened my eyes to show my siblings the awe I felt. But my eyes were drawn to a man walking past German. The shirtless man wore hot pink spandex shorts with a tutu around his knees and super tall pink stilettos. This man's eccentric outfit trumped my love affair with the paella. I smiled as I looked past German, "Oh my gosh. That guy behind you is wearing *quite* the outfit." German turned around to face the man I was talking about, then saw a dozen similarly dressed, or undressed, people who were following the first man. German reacted excitedly, and said, "OMG, is there a Pride parade?" Arelly pulled out her phone from her pocket and googled "Pride parade in Barcelona." She cheered, "Yes! This weekend is the Pride Festival."

We finished our meal and followed the masses until we arrived at the Pride celebration. This was the first Pride festival I'd ever been to. I stood in the middle of the street and saw hundreds of people. Every color of the rainbow adorned attendees' outfits and the surrounding decor. I looked farther down the street and saw something lit up like a stage. Techno music poured out of the stereos that lined the street. I made my way further into the crowd, accompanied by my brother and sister. A circle of people caught my eye. As I neared them, I saw they surrounded several individuals performing stunning tricks with hula hoops. To my right, a man did a backflip. To my left, I saw groups of people dancing the salsa. Everyone smiled and danced. We smiled and laughed with one another. It's moments like these that remind me why my mom always encourages me to travel and to immerse myself in new cultures. It educates you about new things and it allows you to stop and be present in the world around you.

. . .

After our adventures in Barcelona, I hugged German and Arelly goodbye and flew to Morocco, alone. My mom and I had planned to go back to Morocco together; however, her health didn't allow her to come. I hoped to take her to meet my host family from 2015, to meet Mohammed—a man who makes beautiful jewelry—to sit in the garden of a gorgeous park in Rabat, to bring her to my favorite bakery on the side of the road, and much more. I felt guilty enjoying the vacation without her there with me.

I'd never been to a country totally alone before this trip. While I was apprehensive, my Moroccan friends made it a great week. My best friend in Morocco, Mouad, who I'd first met while in Morocco with my mom, asked me to hang out one day. He pulled up to my hotel. I was so excited to see him that I ran out to hug him. "Where are we going?" I asked. He smiled and said, "You'll see."

I climbed into the back of the car and greeted his friend. I couldn't wipe the smile off my face. The car stopped and I looked out the window to see the megamall. I was confused what we might be doing here, but I just followed Mouad. We made our way through the mall crowded with people and running children. The smell of pizza mingled with sushi and Mexican food, a colossal and diverse combination of flavors. I followed him until he stopped outside the indoor ice-skating rink. He looked at me and said, "I remember that last time you were here you told me you wanted to go ice skating, but you didn't have the time. So . . ."

My smile grew and I hugged him fervently. *Damn, he's such a good friend,* I thought to myself. We climbed onto the ice and clumsily made our way around the rink. I awkwardly walked like a toddler taking their first steps. But after a lap or two around, I started getting the hang of it. I skated next to Mouad. As I started getting more confident, I looked down to see my lace untied. At that very instant, the ground fell from beneath me and I ended up face first on the ice. I remained laying there for a moment because my constant laughs kept me from getting up. Mouad helped me up and I continued to laugh.

I left my mom a voice message later that night, "Hey Mama, I miss you. But I'm doing well. My friends here are really taking care of me. I'm happy. See you in a week."

Exactly a week later, I arrived home. I waited for her on the curb at LAX. My body was heavy from exhaustion, so I leaned most of my weight on my bags. I excitedly waited to see my favorite person in the world. She pulled up, and I knew it was her from the license plate that read "GGGGR8FL." If my mom didn't promote the importance of gratitude enough in conversation, her license plate was enough to remind you. I placed my suitcase in the trunk and hopped in the front seat. I never realized until recently how lucky I was to be able to sit in the front seat with my Mama. A "traditional" family places the parents in the front seat and the children behind them, but I was always my mom's equal. I got to sit in the front seat and control the music, navigate, and keep my Mama company.

When we arrived home, I opened the front door and comforted my barking dog, which I do every single time I came home from a trip. When he got over the excitement and laid down, I'd sit on the couch and cuddle with my mom. No matter the hour I arrived home from a trip, whether it was noon, 5:00 p.m., or even 2:00 a.m., my mom would sit on the couch with me as I showed her every single photo I took on my phone throughout the trip and told her *all* the stories. I couldn't wait until the next day; I had to show her right then in the moment.

I was so glad I decided to travel that summer, despite the nervous feeling I carried inside when thinking back to her mini stroke. Considering she was doing relatively well, I felt more comfortable going off to college for my freshman year.

. . .

I survived my first semester at college and felt more secure about my mom's health. Accordingly, I decided I wanted to spend the summer abroad after my first year in college. I applied for several international summer opportunities and received rejection after rejection. However, my mom forwarded me one grant I hadn't considered. I applied and received $3,000 to use for service work in Amman, Jordan. I went home to Los Angeles for a week before going to Jordan to work as an English teacher for a Catholic nonprofit organization.

In my first week, my organization placed me in a classroom of thirty seven-year-old kids without any instruction other than, "Give them an English class."

I was overwhelmed; I'd never taught in a classroom alone before. I looked out at the sea of students sitting at their desks, speaking to one another in a language I didn't understand. The students I served were Syrian refugees, and the dialect they spoke was unique from the Modern Standard Arabic I had learned. I'd come home from work at the end of the day exhausted.

Before I slept, I'd often call my mom. She always knew how to comfort me and also how to guide me despite being thousands of miles away. Over the first few weeks that I stayed in Amman, I became closer and closer with another volunteer who I lived with. He and I would sit on the couch every day after work and talk about everything.

One night, I had to tell my mom on the phone, "Mama—I like my roommate." I paused, "I tried not to . . . but he just makes me so happy." I could hear my mom roll her eyes through the phone.

"Grace, you cannot like your roommate. It's a bad idea. I bet he's amazing, but you just need to learn how to appreciate his friendship and nothing more."

"But Mama!" I jumped in. "What if he likes me too? Should I tell him?"

"If you tell him, it's going to ruin everything. Just enjoy his company. Don't do anything."

I sighed. "You're right . . ."

"I know," she replied. "But other than boys, how's it going?"

I responded, "Actually, I've been feeling frustrated lately. I've been teaching English classes to a bunch of different-aged kids at this one school, but they just throw me into the classrooms without knowing what the students have learned and I feel like I'm just a foreigner they're parading around. I want to do more. I want to do meaningful work, but I don't want to act entitled and tell them what I should be doing; I don't know. It's been great getting to know the students, but I frankly feel useless."

I could hear her take a deep breath. "I'm sorry you're feeling that way. I think you're right that you don't really have the authority to tell them you want something different, but you gotta make do with what you have. It's frustrating that you don't know what level the students are at so you can't create appropriate lesson plans. I know you've been feeling useless lately, and I'm sorry you feel that way. Maybe it will help you deepen your understanding of meaningful service work versus useless service work in the future?"

"You're right, Mama. It's just hard 'cause I want to be doing more, but I'm here to help the organization rather than advance my 'agenda.'"

"That's good you're reflecting on this, Girlie," my mom responded. "You may not be able to change the resources they provide you, but you can change your approach. Think of what you do have control over and plan out what you can do to teach kids English."

"Thanks for the advice, Mama."

It was a challenging summer experience, but I learned a lot. Not only did I learn about what meaningful service looked like, but I also learned how to be comfortable being away from my mom for long periods of time. I took action by always choosing adventure when possible and trusted my mom would be okay. But when I went back to college my sophomore year, that new feeling of relief would be ripped away.

CHAPTER 5

RECOGNIZE THE POWER OF COMMUNITY

———

One month into my second year at Georgetown, one of my best friends, Maddie, stood up from my bed. "I gotta go to sleep! I have to get up early tomorrow." I finished the last kernels of popcorn in my bowl and replied with a full mouth, "Aww. Okay! Thanks for coming over. I'm glad you finally got to see this romcom with me!"

She packed up her bag and walked out of my dorm room. I laid on my bed for a minute longer in the dark. I looked at the twinkly lights surrounding the movie that was projected on my wall. I thought to myself, *I'm really happy.* I got up to tell my Mama what a fun night I had with Maddie. My mom picked up the phone, like she always does, and I spewed out all the joy I was feeling. "Mama! Hi! Oh my god, I just had the best night. Maddie came over and we watched a stupid romcom that made us sob, but it was so fun. We just sat on my bed eating raw cookie dough and we used my projector to watch the movie and it worked so well. OMG, it was so fun. I just love it here. I miss you. How are you, Mama?"

She replied calmly, "I'm fine. Don't freak out, but I've been in the hospital for two days now." My heart dropped. *My mom was in the hospital again? Was she okay? Was it serious? Was she going to be okay? She had been there for two days and she was just telling me now?*

So many thoughts ran through my head and I couldn't control them. I knew I could count on her to be honest, no matter how harsh, so I asked her, "What happened?"

She explained, "I was having shortage of breath and I wasn't sure why, so I came to the doctor and they said I have pneumonia. They took X-rays of my lungs to check if there are any fluids in there." I was blown away by how calm she remained when so many things went wrong.

I was not calm and immediately said, "Do you need me to come home? I can come home this weekend. Are you okay?"

"Take a breath. I'm fine. You don't need to come home; they're just handling everything. I have the Big Kids taking care of me. I'm just tired."

She hung up and my mind filled with thoughts about my mom. I tried to study, but after reading the same sentence five times, I realized I couldn't focus. It didn't help that one of the most stressful times regarding my mom's health coincided with my most academically rigorous semester at Georgetown. Not only was I taking a full class load, but I also had a part-time job and was a Residential Assistant (RA). I sucked up my feelings and carried on for a couple days.

Four days after the surprise news from my mom, she called to tell me she was discharged from the hospital. That brought me a wave of relief. But only three days after she was discharged—after I thought the health scare was behind us—she called me again.

"Hey, Girlie." Her voice sounded notably weaker. "I wanted to let you know that I'm in the hospital again . . . I was having trouble breathing, and they said I have double pneumonia. They say there is fluid in both of my lungs that's making it hard to breathe."

My eyes welled with tears. "O . . . Oh . . . Okay." Chills covered my skin, and my teeth began to chatter. My teeth chatter every time I get nervous. But I also knew she was strong and she'd endured a lot of medical shit. I checked in with my mom by calling her every single day. I noted a change in her energy level. I felt hopeful, until I talked to my mom's colleague and my family friend, Patrick. He told me, "She doesn't seem like herself. Her skin looks pale and slightly yellow. She's not being sarcastic or making fun of me." This was most concerning because she was usually the life of the party. She'd tease everyone and make jokes!

I went to my friend Tommy and told him everything. I knocked on his door and he opened it to see my face—with furrowed brows of worry. He let me in, and I started, "I just . . . She's been in the hospital twice in one month. That's not good . . . That's *not* good. Oh god. I'm just . . ." I trailed on, unsure of what I was trying to say. He sat there listening attentively and offered supportive silence; I just needed to rant.

When the words flowing out of me stopped, he affirmed my emotions and said, "That sucks! I'm sorry." People often pity their friends when they're sad or they try to make them feel better instantly, but I appreciated that Tommy knew how to affirm my feelings where I was at.

Little did I know her health would worsen, and she'd spend two weeks in a hospital bed.

I tried so hard to focus on my classes. I wanted to get good grades to keep up my GPA, but thoughts of my mom distracted me. I did not do well on any of my assignments. Once in economics class, I felt so overwhelmed that I couldn't help but fall asleep in class. I tried to learn, I wanted to listen, but it felt like the world was crashing down around me. My nights were filled with nightmares about my mom. I was taking an intensive Arabic course and the professor was extremely critical of my work and strict about grammar. Even when I tried to be perfect, she always found some small mistake, so I gave up. I didn't have the energy to fight back. My thoughts were consumed by my mom.

If that weren't enough, my mom called me one day from the hospital with another update about her dear friend and my other godmother, Donna.

"Hey Gracie Girl," she said, "remember how Donna was having that numbness before you went to school?"

"Yes, I remember." I replied with a shaky voice.

"She has a brain tumor."

I gripped my phone tightly until my knuckles turned white. *Donna has brain cancer? Donna, my godmother, who always eats healthy, never has dessert, and exercises regularly? I'd never had someone I knew impacted by cancer, but now it was happening. I can't lose her.*

Donna is my cheerleader. I understand that my mom had to be critical of me, but Donna always complimented me on everything I did. Once, several years ago, Donna pulled me aside after we had dinner at her house. During the meal, my mom had criticized me. Donna sat down with me at the table and held my hand. "Aww, Gracie. I'm sorry that your mama is tough on you. If you were my daughter, I'd never complain. You're the perfect child." My vision blurred from the tears welling in my eyes. I leaned my head against Donna's chest while she brushed her fingers through my hair and rubbed my back. "I wish my mom thought that, too," I said while looking up at Donna.

I remember her loving words often, so when my mom told me Donna had cancer, I could hardly breathe. *I can't lose my mom. I can't lose my godmother, too.* I didn't know if Donna would recover through chemotherapy. I also didn't know how long my mom would be in the hospital.

A few days after my mom called me with this update, I was in a one-on-one meeting with my supervisor, and I completely spaced out. My supervisor called out my name. "Grace!" I didn't hear him until he asked me, "Grace, what do you need?" I thought back to the lesson my mom had taught me, "Ask and you shall receive."

I looked down at my knuckles that were white from my angry fist, then glanced up at him with devastated eyes. I thought about what I needed. As I thought about my mom and how much I missed her and wished I could be with her, a tear rolled down my cheek. I wanted to yell out loud, "I just want to be with my Mama!" But I had to think about school. I took a moment to breathe and discern what I really needed. My mom was always so good at identifying what she needed, but she told me she gained that skill through deep reflection and discernment. I looked up at my supervisor with tears in my eyes and said, "I need to go home . . . but I can't."

He took a deep breath and said, "Let's look at your calendar and find a way to get you home." He sat with me for thirty minutes talking me through the steps, so I could fly home to be with my Mama. He planned out an adjusted work schedule and helped me email my academic dean. Now I see why my mom tells me to ask for what I need: sometimes, you might just get it.

I flew home to Los Angeles that weekend to be with my Mama. She was moved from the hospital to rehab to regain her strength after she'd been in a hospital bed for more than two weeks. I skipped into the room happy to see her. Then my gaze focused on the several IVs in her arm and a walker next to her bed. I slowly dropped all my bags off in the corner of the room next to the La-Z-Boy chair that would be my bed for the next two nights. I walked back to my Mama and crawled into her hospital bed to snuggle. She touched my face and a tear fell off my face into her palm. I needed to be close to her again. I also noticed the color had returned to her face.

She mentioned she had started dialysis in rehab. It was making her feel better. I felt mixed about the news. I was happy that dialysis was improving her day-to-day, but I was anxious knowing that once you start dialysis, the only way to get off of it is by having a kidney transplant. It had been more than ten years since her first kidney transplant, and I was not ready to think of her going through that again.

"Mama! Tonight is going to be a *fun* night," I declared. "How about I go out and get dinner, then I bring it back and we can eat dinner with a movie?"

She smiled, "That would be lovely."

. . .

I headed out to the nearest store and bought salami, breadsticks, mozzarella, and fruit. I pulled up a chair next to her bed and placed the adjustable table between us. I carefully laid out our picnic on the hospital bedside table. We made little salami and cheese and cracker sandwiches and closed our eyes, pretending that we were back in Italy again. We sat there munching, laughing, and exchanging stories. It was as if she wasn't in a hospital bed and as if I hadn't flown out because she was sick, but rather to have a fun weekend together. I put away the picnic and crawled back into her bed, placing the computer on my lap to prepare our romcom for the evening. I don't even remember what we watched, all I know is I felt safe again and I felt everything was going to be okay. We managed to have fun together regardless of the shitty circumstances.

The next day, we reserved the conference room in the rehabilitation center to celebrate Arelly's birthday. German, Ale, and Arelly arrived for the birthday party. Ale brought a chocolate ice cream cake to celebrate, and I brought a few colorful candles to put on top. When it came time to sing, German pulled out his lighter and leaned over the cake to light the candles, but all of a sudden, a nurse burst through the door and yelled, "You cannot light a candle in this building! There is extra oxygen in the building that could make a match cause an explosion!" She left and we all looked like little kids who had gotten into trouble. Then Arelly started laughing and we all joined in. We thought of a rehab center catching on fire from a *fricking* birthday candle.

. . .

On November 5, I sang into the phone, "Happy birthday, Mama! So, what are you doing for your birthday?"

"Oh, you know! Just dinner with the Big Kids at a BBQ restaurant. Should be yummy," she shared. "Oh! I forgot to ask. Can you do something for me?" I was all ears because she rarely asked me for favors. "I'm asking for a kidney for my birthday this year." She divulged. "Can you help me with my Facebook post? And then can you write your own post about it on your wall?"

"Of course, Mama," I replied.

We sat on the phone together drafting her "Kidney Ask" for her birthday wish. On November 5, 2018, she wrote on her Facebook:

"My birthday wish: a new kidney donor! After eleven years, the kidney Joanne graciously donated has slowly stopped working. I'm now on dialysis three times a week until I find a living donor. That limits my life in so many ways. If you have ever thought of donating a kidney, or even if you haven't, please consider seeing if you are a potential match. The folks at Cedar Sinai will be happy to talk to you about what it entails."

After we posted, three things happened:

1. One hundred and one people shared her post.
2. So many people called the hospital that they told my mom to stop telling people to call because there was too much interest.
3. Anthony, an ex-coworker of my mom's, saw my Facebook post and was one of the callers who ended up being my mom's kidney donor.

So many people wanted to donate their kidney to my mom! Individuals who she had worked with, my closest friends, my sister, and even a couple students I know at Georgetown who had never met my mom called the hospital to leave their name. It was incredible. As my mom would say, "It's the power of community." Many people may think my mom had to raise me alone, but my mom said, "I was never alone because I had my village to support me." During her various surgeries and medical situations during 2018 through 2020, we had a group chat called "Pam's Village," in which she would give important updates about her health and ask for peoples' help in terms of bringing her meals at home during recovery or sneaking real food into the hospital ("not the crap" that they gave her).

My mom believed in the power of community and surrounded herself with the best of people; thus, when she asked her community for what she needed, she received two donor kidneys in her lifetime.

While my mom sought a kidney to save her from regular dialysis visits, Donna's tumor grew larger despite the chemotherapy she underwent and the steroids she took. It was hard to think beyond the present moment, with my mom's health unstable and my godmother's health declining. However, my mom encouraged me to move forward and apply for grants so I could work internationally in the summer of my sophomore year. One fellowship, called GU Impacts, accepted me to their program and gave me the opportunity to work for Women for Women International in Sarajevo, Bosnia and Herzegovina, for the whole summer. I was thrilled to find a fully sponsored program because, as my mom told me, I could travel wherever I wanted as long as she didn't have to pay for any of it. I took that lesson as far as it would go and asked my mom if I could also study abroad in the fall of my junior year in Chile.

There was so much adventure to be had, but I still had my reservations, especially with Donna's health declining and my mom doing dialysis three times a week. If I decided to participate in both programs, I would be traveling for six months straight with only one week at home in between Bosnia and Chile. I had to decide between my mom and pursuing adventure and deepening my education. If I went, I'd gain international experience, enhance my language skills, and develop my independence; however, if I went and something happened to my mom, I'd never forgive myself for not being with her. If I stayed, my mom would be angry that I'd given up a chance to travel to do nothing at home with her.

Ultimately, I decided to accept the fellowship in Sarajevo and study abroad in Chile and Argentina with the full support of my mom. The next six months were unforgettable.

CHAPTER 6

LEARN FROM STRANGERS

———

It was 4:00 a.m. and I was still packing my bags. The journey to Bosnia and Herzegovina begins in three hours, but I'm a last-minute packer. I sat on the floor surrounded by various piles of clothing. I looked over and saw my suitcase open and empty. My mom laid in my bed under the covers asleep with the lights on and the fan buzzing. She knew I liked the company while I packed for trips. She wasn't deep in sleep, so I urged, "Hey Mama, ask me if I have certain things. Quiz me."

She hummed herself out of her light nap and opened her eyes, "Uh, let's see. Portable charger?"

"Check!" I responded.

"Water bottle?"

"Check."

"Copies of passport?"

"Check."

"*Point to It* book?"

"Yup!"

My mom gave me a small book for Christmas called *Point to It*. The booklet is filled with tons of pictures that can be used when traveling in a country where I don't speak the language. She told me to take it to Bosnia and point to the picture that I need when trying to communicate with someone.

I zipped up my bag, stuffed my backpack, and hopped in the car. I gave my Mama a huge hug and a kiss before I departed on my twelve-week journey.

. . .

I arrived at the door of my new home in Sarajevo, Bosnia and Herzegovina. The cement entryway to the apartment was covered with graffiti and there were bullet holes in the building exterior left over from the war that happened twenty years ago. Only ten steps away from my apartment was the spot where Archduke Ferdinand was assassinated. For the history buffs, you know. For others, this assassination was the spark that began World War I.

I entered the building and climbed four flights of cement stairs. After what felt like climbing Mount Everest, I was face-to-face with the doorknob. I stood outside for two minutes catching my breath. I reached for the key in my pocket and opened the white wooden doors to find a beautiful entryway with hardwood floors, a full-length mirror, and a gorgeous Bosnian rug. I opened another set of doors to find a living room that smelled like dust. Behind the velvet couch were several large windows, through which I could see the gorgeous Miljacka River that goes through the center of Sarajevo. Amidst the dusk, one spectacular sight caught my eye. A stunning black mosque stood tall with its minaret scratching the sky. The sun went to sleep behind the silhouettes of buildings across from the river. As the city darkened, windows lit up like fireflies in the night.

I made my way into a second living room with furniture just as lovely and antique as the first room. Then I walked into the bedroom that would be my home for the next two and half months. My heartbeat quickened as I thought anxiously about all the good or bad that was yet to come during my time in Sarajevo. But one thing I knew, and loved, was that my mom had somehow found this apartment on a Bosnian real estate website, so I felt she was already part of the journey. My mom taught me the importance of learning about other cultures and immersing yourself fully, so I prepared myself for the coming weeks of intense immersion.

The two first weeks were terrible. Every friend I found was only in town for a couple of days. Adjusting to my new job was hard because it was my first time working forty hours per week. I didn't speak any Bosnian and few people spoke English, so I felt very lonely. I joined a Facebook group called Expats in Sarajevo and went out on three different coffee meetups with different girls living in Sarajevo, hoping I could find a best friend. I called my mom one night when I couldn't bear to go out on one more "friend date." I was socialized out.

"Hey, Mama."

"Hey, Girlie. How's it going?" she replied.

"I'm . . . I'm . . . I'm just so tired, Mama. I can't understand what anyone is saying at work, I don't have any friends, and I'm just exhausted. Today, I even climbed a mountain to check out a hostel in hopes of meeting some cool people, but no one was there. I'm just so tired. I wish I could find people who were actually staying and working in Sarajevo instead of people just on vacation. I've met up with a few people from the Facebook page, but no one was the right person for me. I just don't know what to do. I miss you." This was rare of me to get homesick. Usually when my mom and I travel, we go to South America because we both speak Spanish, or I go to an Arabic speaking country because I speak some Arabic; however, this was the first time I was living in a country where I didn't speak the language at *all*.

My mom calmly took a breath to make sure I was finished, then replied, "I'm sorry, Girlie. I miss you too. Well, let's think where would people who work in Bosnia go? Where could you find people who live there and aren't just visiting?" She paused to think while I just laid in my bed, defeated and not eager to try to make any new friends. Then she said, "What if you took a language class?" She continued, "You could learn how to communicate with locals and there might be expatriates in the class if they're planning to stay for a while." My mom knows me so well. I love learning languages and enrolling in a language class would make it easier for me to immerse myself in the culture.

"Good idea, Mama. I'll ask around."

Five seconds later, my mom already had something: "I just sent you a link to a language school I found. Maybe go visit the school and check it out before signing up?"

"Thanks, Mama. I love you."

"Love you too, Girlie. Let me know how it goes."

I hung up and felt a swell of emotions rise in my chest—a combination of excitement and nervousness.

Two weeks later, I enrolled in an intensive Bosnian course for three hours every day after work for three weeks. I went into the class trying to make friends and came out of the class speaking intermediate Bosnian. My mom again showed me not to freak out, but instead take a moment to reflect, breathe, and then use my resources to find a solution.

On the first day of the course, I felt out of my element. Some students already knew the teachers and I didn't. In the room, there were fifteen of us coming from Canada, the United States, Greece, Japan, Switzerland, Mexico, the United Kingdom, the Czech Republic, Sweden, or Germany—all present with the goal of immersing ourselves more into the Sarajevo community. The first week's theme was theater, so we spent the first hour of class watching a Bosnian film, then taking the same script and acting scenes out. I love theater and acting, so this activity was exhilarating. One classmate also loved acting, so he and I became the extroverts of the class. I noticed one American girl in the intermediate class had missed three days of classes, so I asked her what happened.

"I've had migraines since the first day of class, so I took a break. I think I need to move to the beginner class." I tried to hide my excitement. I kept my lips together in a half smile. If she came to the beginner class, she would be with me. I noticed her out of all the other students because she had a good sense of humor and had a little sass, which I appreciated. Over the next two weeks, this girl, Abby, became my best friend.

The first time we hung out, I was nervous because I was so desperate to find a good friend. But then I realized we were scarily similar. She grew up in rural Ohio, is from a family of five, and was working in Bosnia as a missionary, whereas I grew up in Los Angeles, come from a family of two, and was working for Women for Women International—we understood each other. We finished each other's sentences and took care of each other. My mom taught me to love the people who need the most love, and when I met Abby, I could tell she was a caretaker like myself, so I knew she needed someone to love and support her. What's beautiful was that she did the same for me, and that's why we've stayed friends since. Abby was the friend I needed to immerse myself more deeply into the culture. She, like me, loved talking to strangers.

Whereas most parents teach their children, "Stranger danger! Don't talk to strangers," my mom said, "You can always learn something from others."

After a few visits to a coffee shop near my work, I began talking to one of the workers in my broken Bosnian language. *Ciao, ja sam Grace, kako si zoveš?* or "Hello, I'm Grace, what's your name?"

He looked up from the cash register with a startled look on his face. He chuckled and responded, *Ja sam Alem. Drago mi je* or "I'm Alem. Nice to meet you."

Each time I came back to the coffee shop, I'd look for Alem just so I could practice my Bosnian and get to know him. I came so often that I developed a rhythm. Each time I would come into the shop, make eye contact with Alem, then ask him, *Šta ima novo?* or "What's new?" He'd reply, while making someone else's drink, *Ništa, ništa. i ti?* or "Nothing, nothing. And you?" When I got to the cashier, he'd ask, *Da li želiš isto?* or "Do you want the same?" and after I nodded and replied with "please" in Bosnian, he would go and make my regular drink. Then he'd often ask me something I completely didn't understand. I'd look back at him bashfully with confused eyes and reply, *Ne rezumijem* or "I don't understand." He laughed and said the same thing again but slowly with added hand gestures. His effort made me smile because I appreciated the lengths he went to support my understanding.

Abby and I visited the coffee shop every day and met each person who worked there. We practiced our Bosnian and they practiced their English. When some workers had a break, they would sit with us and chat in Bosnian until we put on our confused faces. Then they would use the limited English they knew until we understood. One worker refused to speak English with us even though she spoke some because she wanted us to practice.

This was one of the rituals I had while living in Bosnia. I'd get coffee and chat with my friends every morning at seven o'clock, then I'd go to my office only a block away and work on grants and marketing until lunchtime. Then, my coworkers and I would take a break for coffee, tell stories, and laugh together. It was incredible what taking a Bosnian class could do. At the beginning, work was exhausting because I couldn't communicate well with my coworkers. After my three-week class, while I wasn't fluent, I could tell jokes to my coworkers, understand their jokes (sometimes), and most importantly, they taught me how to curse—essential survival skills when learning a language.

I went to sleep smiling and woke up excited to do it all again. I found more expatriates through a weekly meetup and thus had people to go to concerts or dancing with. I even made friends with the manager of a travel company near my house. Some days I would stop by her office to chat with her because she made me laugh. I bought a ticket to go to a music festival in the forest, but needed a tent to sleep in. I shared my concern, and my friend replied, "Don't worry Grace. I'll get you a tent. I'll just buy one and you can use it." Her generosity blew me away.

One Friday afternoon at three o'clock, my boss told me to take the next week off. She told me, "Grace. I know you want to travel, but the weekend is not long enough, so take next week to go to every place you want to visit."

A look of excitement glowed on my face and I ran down to the coffee shop to plan the trip ASAP. Who do I call when I need help planning for travel? Of course, my mom.

"Hey, Mama! Can you chat?" I asked.

"Of course!" She remarked. "I'm in dialysis, so it's perfect timing." My mom started dialysis again in the fall of 2018 for the first time in eleven years. Three times a week, she had to go to a medical center for three hours each session so the machine could clean her blood better than her current kidneys could. Before dialysis, she had lost her taste and smell, which made dining out less fun. But funny, sometimes. She couldn't taste, so every time we went out, she'd ask the waiter, "What has the best texture? Do you have a dish with a lot of different textures?" I was used to the question, but the waiter's face every time was priceless. The waiter wrinkled his brow and looked up for a moment considering why this woman would ask this question, but then would quickly reply, "Uhh. Let me ask the chef and get back to you." The waiter probably ran to read the menu looking for the crunchiest dish!

Dialysis was the best time to talk to my mom because she was hooked up to the machine and all she could do was be on her phone or nap.

"So . . ." I continued. "I have all of next week off from work. I want to go to six countries in nine days. Will you help me?"

"Let's do it!" She cheered.

I spent four hours on the phone with my mom in the coffee shop while we simultaneously looked for bus tickets and hostels. It was 7:30 a.m. for my mom and 3:30 p.m. for me.

I started, "Okay, so I want to go to Serbia, Bulgaria, Macedonia, Albania, Montenegro, and Croatia. I don't want to pay to fly because that's expensive. My budget is $500 for the whole trip. I'll just stay in hostels and I'll walk places instead of taking a taxi."

"Okay, Girlie. Are you going with anyone?"

"Nope."

"That's alright. You'll be fine." She paused "I found this website that offers pretty cheap bus trips between some Balkan countries; I'll send it to you now."

Sure enough, in the two minutes I had been explaining my trip ideas, my mom was simultaneously browsing the internet for Balkan bus companies. Always getting stuff done. Her health had been unstable since our trip to Puerto Rico, and she hadn't been able to travel since. "I love getting to live through your travels," she told me. "I miss traveling."

I responded, "I miss traveling with you, Mama!"

I hadn't taken time to reflect on how much I missed traveling with her. I recalled memories of exploring downtown Cuzco, Peru, with her at night, discovering delicious bakeries in Italy, people-watching while eating churros in Havana, Cuba, riding in a boat in Bocas del Toro, Panama, or even taking a *tuk tuk* to get ice cream with her in Phnom Penh, Cambodia. I missed the adventures, and I missed her companionship. Traveling is fun, don't get me wrong, but it's nice having your mom there to joke with, pay for food, look for tours, and snuggle with you at the end of a long-ass day.

It didn't hit me until I arrived by bus to my first city: Belgrade. I called my mom. But she didn't pick up. I left an audio message for her on WhatsApp:

"Hey, Mama. I just wanted to say thank you. I want to tell you I'm grateful you're my mom because most parents wouldn't let their child go backpacking for a week to random countries they'd never been to . . . I don't know why it hit me today. Maybe it was because this is my first time traveling alone, truly alone, without knowing anyone. I'm confident in my ability to figure things out because you taught me how to be resourceful. Anyway, I'm not trying to be sappy, but I just wanted to say thanks for trusting me to go on these adventures. I love you, Mama. Okay, Bye!"

Remember when I told you my mom supported me talking to strangers? Just the first night I was in Belgrade, Serbia, I met a British guy sitting on the fortress wall. We sat in silence. I could feel the hardness of the cement under me, but I never grew uncomfortable because the sights were so spectacular. The sun fell from the sky into a painting of orange and pink and purple. The sun shone into my eyes as it set, but I didn't mind. It felt so good being a solo traveler exploring the world. The colors of the sunset reflected off of the water below.

My thoughts were interrupted by two kids chasing each other and laughing on the path below where I sat. Once brought back to reality, I noticed the guy next to me and couldn't stay quiet. I'd gone a whole day traveling alone, and while it was fun, I missed having a buddy to talk to about life. "Excuse me," I said with a shake in my voice, "Do you speak English?" He turned his head to figure out who had interrupted his sunset experience. "Uh. Yeah. I do." He had a kind face. There was also a subtle look in his face that begged the question, "Who is this person and what does she want?"

I took that as my cue to start a conversation, "Where are you from?"

"England, and you?"

I told him a bit about myself and asked what he was doing in Serbia. He introduced himself as Stephen, then told me he'd taken a break from work just to travel for a week.

"You're lucky you live in Europe! You could go to a different country every weekend if you wanted!" Our conversation went on and I quite enjoyed him as a conversation partner. I then told him about this app that connects travelers with one another and asked if he'd join me at one of the meetups that I'd found in Belgrade. Feeling adventurous, he accepted my offer. He and I left the fortress together and walked around in search of a good restaurant where we could meet other travelers.

After we found a great restaurant, we invited other travelers. While we'd all met only minutes before, the fact that we were all solo travelers gave us something in common. We were all hungry for companionship which made the conversation more fun and entertaining. Then another tall and pale man approached the table awkwardly, "Is this the Couchsurfing meetup?" We affirmed him with a roar of laughter and smiles. When he sat, I looked more carefully, and I couldn't shake something that convinced me that I'd met him before. I pushed the thought aside.

Stephen and I were at one end of the table and couldn't stop laughing. We had the same sense of humor, so we just kept teasing one another. Stephen told me about his job in education. I listened attentively. He taught me a lot about the best practices of interacting with children and gave me tips on how to motivate students without being condescending. I tried focusing on our conversation, but I couldn't help but look back at the man who recently arrived. I paused. "Do I know you? I feel like we've met." I inquired.

He looked at me with a wrinkled brow, "Um, you look familiar too. I just came from Bosnia."

"I work in Bosnia. Were you on the Srebrenica tour with Funky Tours?"

I realized he and I had gone on the same tour only a couple weeks earlier. It's a small world. And this is why I talk to strangers. My mom taught me to connect with every person I meet because they may be able to teach you something, or better yet, they may show you something new.

On the fourteen-hour bus ride from North Macedonia to Tirana, Albania, I met two Albanian men who spoke some Bosnian, so we connected. We made jokes the whole bus ride. At 4:00 a.m., the driver stopped at a pit stop. My new friends told me to get off the bus and eat breakfast with them. I would have never known what an Albanian breakfast was, but thanks to them, I learned that a breakfast consists of two huge piles of rice, shredded meat, and some dairy sauce poured on top.

At the end of my experience in the Balkans, I went to Turkey for a week at my mom's recommendation. I was especially excited to go on a hot air balloon ride in the city of Cappadocia because it's known as the best city in the world to go on a hot air balloon. Unfortunately, the wind was too strong, so we couldn't ride one for any of the three days we were there. I was disappointed. However, I decided to make the most of my time and invited some other girls I'd met to go on an ATV tour around the mountains and valleys of Cappadocia. It wasn't the same as hot air ballooning, but it was a blast.

On my last night in Istanbul, I went to visit a traditional Turkish tea shop and met a worker. He didn't speak much English and I apologized that I didn't speak Turkish, but he replied he actually spoke Arabic.

I responded, *Sahih? Min ayna anta?* or "Really? Where are you from?"

Ana min al Maghrib or "I am from Morocco," he responded with a smile on his face. *Mashallah! Ana ohibu al Maghrib. Dhabtu ila al Maghrib 4 marat. Hiya beladi al mufadala,* or "Bless the lord! I love Morocco. I've been there four times. It's my favorite country," I exclaimed. His face lit up with a smile. All the colors in the shop displays seemed brighter. He excitedly moved from behind the counter and invited me to take a seat at one of the tables in the shop. He brought me some delicious Turkish apple tea and asked me more about my experience in Morocco. He asked me who my favorite Moroccan singer was, and we sat there singing Moroccan pop songs! It was such a lovely interaction. At the end of the conversation, I packed up several Turkish delights to bring home and share with my family.

Finally, after four months, I arrived home. You may imagine my homecoming as therapeutic and calming; however, when I came home from college, my mom postponed all of her doctor's appointments for the week so we could do everything together—and I mean *everything.* We spent several hours at the police department waiting for the clearance needed for my Chilean visa, then we spent two more hours at a store looking for snacks and gifts for my host families, and then we arrived home late at night and collapsed in exhaustion.

My Mama and I would unwind watching *New Girl* or *Gilmore Girls* because both made us laugh. Those were my favorite nights. We didn't care what we were watching; we just wanted each other's company. We always had so much fun together when I came home from trips or college. Since her health prevented her from traveling, only a couple days after I arrived home from Turkey, my mom and I had a staycation in Santa Monica—only 20 minutes from our house—because it gave us the time to truly relax, go swimming, or snuggle in bed while we watched a dumb romcom.

One night, we watched a movie together on my mom's bed. I remember pausing. I forgot about the movie and looked at the blue light reflecting from the computer onto my mom's face. She was fast asleep; she could never make it through an entire movie without falling asleep. Her subtle snore continued. Her mouth was parted slightly, and the only sound audible except her snore was the hum of the air conditioner. I felt so grateful to be on this little vacation with my Mama and it made me so happy to see her sleep since she was always working. I turned off the computer and sneakily crawled out of her bed and into my own.

All things come to an end, and only one week after returning to Los Angeles, I was off to South America for my semester abroad. I finally trusted my mom's health to be stable and hoped that Donna would recover, but that was the farthest from the truth. The next few months would be the beginning of my year in hell.

CHAPTER 7

LOVE THOSE WHO NEED THE MOST LOVE

———

Two weeks into my time in Santiago, Chile, I met my host family: Sussi and Gaspar, a single mom and her eight-year-old son. Although the program assigned me to the host family, we chose to grow as close as we did because both Sussi and I needed someone to talk to. My favorite part of the day was doing dishes with Sussi after dinner. Gaspar played with toys in the living room while she and I stood in front of the sink. One night, she picked up a plate, causing it to clink against the others, and brought it to the sink. She grabbed the sponge and lathered it with soap. I leaned over and asked her about her job. Sussi worked as a school counselor and was a single mom—two full-time jobs. I inquired, *¿Cómo fue tú día en la escuela?* "How was your day at school?" She paused with the sponge in her hand and took a deep breath. After living with her for a month, I was able to read her body language. "What happened?" I asked.

"It was so busy. I had back-to-back meetings with students because so many parents requested that I check in with their kids. I'm just so tired."

She returned to scrubbing the plates. I waited patiently as I dried the clean ones. Growing up with a single mom, I knew how much my mom needed to unload at the end of the day. Having an eight-year-old son, Sussi only had her mom to check in with her about her day, so I was more than happy to be a sounding board for her. My Mama gave me the ability to see who needs the most love, and then deliver love to that person. I could see how tired she was, but like my mom, she persevered.

She finished her unloading of the day and asked me about me and my friends. I replied, "I just don't feel close with any of the students in the cohort, so I'm trying to make my own Chilean friends. Today, I met a group of students in one of the seminars, and they're really funny! They invited me to have lunch with them and we had such a great time." She passed me the last plate with a smile, and said in Spanish, "I'm so glad you found people you can hang out with."

Sussi was more like a best friend than a mom to me; she reminded me of my godmother Donna. Like Donna, Sussi would talk with me about boys who I liked in a giggly, girly way. Like Donna, Sussi constantly told me what a hard worker and good person I am. Like Donna, Sussi loved wine. I was grateful that when I missed Donna most, God sent me Sussi.

One night my mom called me. I was lying in my bed wrapped up in two wool blankets to combat the cold night in Chile. Then I heard the buzz of my phone moving against the dresser and I saw the blue light from my phone illuminate the room. Once I saw "Mama Rector" on the screen, I answered it immediately.

"Hey, Mama."

"Hey, Girlie."

"How are you doing?"

"I'm okay. How are you?"

Not clueing into the tone of her voice, I rattled on about all the events of the day and all the people I had met.

"Hey, Girlie, I need to tell you something about Donna."

"Mmhmm," I said, trying not to waiver with my voice.

"I talked to her nurse today. They're going to stop radiation. The nurse said that . . ." I heard my Mama's voice crack, then I heard her take a deep breath. "She only has about three to six weeks to live."

My heart dropped.

I said nothing. A tear fell down my face and I held my breath so a sob wouldn't erupt. This was the first moment I realized Donna was not going to get better. The last time I hugged Donna, my mom told me to say goodbye because it may be the last time. I know my mom always tells me the truth even if it's hard to hear—but I wish she would just lie and say, *"Everything is going to be okay."*

My shoulders shook, and my vision blurred. I couldn't stop crying.

"You okay, Girlie?" my mom asked.

A wail came out of me like nothing I've ever heard before. I gasped for air and my mouth fell open in despair. My mom heard my sobs and simply said, "Oh, my Girlie." I began to pace the room. "Oh . . . my . . . God. This can't be happening," I murmured. My sobs echoed so loudly, I was scared I would wake Sussi and Gaspar. My mom and I exchanged cries over the phone and dared not say anything for a long time. I gripped the phone tightly and curled my toes, consumed by hatred for the world that would allow her to die.

Finally, when I was able to catch my breath, I asked, "Did you tell Kate?" Donna would leave me, but she would also leave behind her seventeen-year-old daughter, Kate. Kate and I grew up as sisters and spent every holiday and birthday together. She and I were inseparable as kids, but distance strained our relationship now. She needed her mom, and since I wasn't there for her physically, I wondered who she would lean on.

"I asked Kate if she wanted to visit Donna again, but she said her last visit was so good she doesn't want to see her mom as she is right now. I bet it's scary for her. The brain tumor has limited Donna's ability to communicate, and she can hardly move. She's just gone mentally."

"Oh, Kate." I couldn't imagine the sadness she would be experiencing.

In the morning, I asked Sussi for a hug. I just needed a familiar touch—crying over the phone wasn't enough for me. Sussi was my family in Chile, and I needed her. Despite the uncertainty of Donna's health, the world went on around me. I took my body to class every day, but my mind and heart were in Los Angeles, thinking of Donna.

At lunch, I sat with my friends Alejandra, Javiera, and Karina. They made me laugh and helped me forget about the bad things, even for just a little while. Alejandra's birthday approached, and she invited me. I arrived at the party with Karina, and we were greeted with smiles and hugs. The highlight of the celebration was the food. We ate delicious *completos,* a traditional Chilean food. A *completo* is a hot dog with mashed avocado, tomatoes, ketchup, mayo, and sometimes chile on top. After I finished my first completo, I couldn't help but reach for another. We sat around the table laughing as the TV hummed in the background. While I knew my girlfriends,

I got to meet new people. Javiera said, "Grace, come play this game with us." She placed a cup right-side-up on top of a liter bottle of Coca Cola. She tapped the bottom of the cup and flipped it, so the opening of the cup landed right on top of the bottle. I was impressed! We all spent the next two hours trying to land it as well as Javiera. Eventually the floor was covered with cups from failed attempts.

Spending time with friends helped me focus on the good rather than the bad. The study abroad program took us to visit schools in Buenos Aires, Argentina, for two weeks, but only two days after our arrival in Argentina, protests erupted in Santiago. Protests started in response to the rise in metro prices, government corruption, and poor quality of education. I stayed in touch with my Chilean friends but felt terrible that I couldn't be with them during this important and difficult time. Little did I know that the protests would last for several months, meaning we wouldn't be able to return to Chile.

After a couple days in Argentina, my mom went into surgery. Her kidney donor, Anthony, was a match; however, before she could receive his kidney, the doctors needed to remove her two polycystic kidneys to make room for the new healthy one. I sat in my lecture in Buenos Aires, anxiously awaiting a text from my mom saying the surgery went well. I heard the hum of the professor speaking, and I wrote down words on my paper, but my mind was focused on my Mama. *It's been so many hours, and I haven't heard anything! What if the surgery didn't go well? What if they couldn't take them out? What if they won't be able to do the transplant after all?* But then I paused and breathed. I recalled how my mom managed to stay calm throughout all the highs and lows of life without panicking. I breathed deeply and turned my attention back to the professor.

Then I heard my phone buzz. It was Margaret, my mom's best friend. Her message read, "She's awake, but she's still in some pain. Do you want to talk to her?" I instantly excused myself from the class and went outside to call my Mama.

She picked up after a few rings. "Hi, Mama!"

"Hey, Girlie," she said in a weak voice. My mom is the strongest person I know with the highest pain tolerance I have ever witnessed, so hearing her voice as weak as it sounded was scary.

"How are you feeling?"

"Last night was really bad. I was in so much pain that Margaret spent the night. I think the nurse just didn't give me pain meds early on enough to prevent the pain. So, it was constantly hurting. I feel better now. They've given me more oxycodone, but it still doesn't feel great."

"I'm sorry, Mama. I wish I was with you."

"Me too, Girlie."

"Did the surgery go well?"

"Yes! They said it went well, but you'll never believe it. They said that the polycystic kidneys were each the size of a watermelon! The doctor told me how big they were, and I asked him if each were the same as individual-sized watermelons or party-sized watermelons, and he said party size. Dang! Now I'll be skinny."

"Wow. That's huge. I bet that's gonna take a lot of pressure off your back. I'm glad they did it though."

"I just sent you a picture of the incision. It's not bad considering how big the kidneys were."

My phone dinged, and I saw a huge red and purple incision on her tummy. Not only was she always honest, but she never protected me from scary pictures of scars or injuries—even if it made me nauseous.

"Dang mom! Ouchy, ouchy, ouchy," I continued. "Well, I'm glad Margaret is with you."

"Me too!" Margaret yelled over the speakerphone.

I paused, then asked, ". . . and how's Donna?"

"She's not doing good. She's not responsive anymore. The nurse says she will pass away in the coming days."

The tears came again. I just couldn't fathom Donna not being there when I came home. I couldn't imagine the smart, witty, and brilliant Donna, unable to articulate a sentence.

My mom heard my little sobs and said, "Aw, Girlie. I'm sorry."

"It's okay."

"Sorry Girlie, but the doctor just came in; I have to go. I love you!"

"Okay Mama, love you more than you can ever say or do or text or email."

"Love you most! I win," She chuckled lightly. We often had this little competition of who could love the other more.

I wiped my eyes with my sleeve, not caring that some mascara ran down my cheek, and walked back into the classroom. Except when I walked back in, there were four middle-aged women. I forgot; it was time to meet our host families. I fell into line as our program director announced the host family pairings. It was then that I met Gabi.

Gabi and I quickly became close. She was also a single mom like Sussi, Donna, and my mom. But Gabi's daughter was my age, so she was also off in college. Home with Gabi felt close to home with my Mama because it was just the two of us. Gabi was the most amazing chef. She would have the deepest conversations with me about politics, boys, life, or whatever was on my mind. She even brought me to her girlfriend's house for one of their friend reunions where everyone brings a different type of tart and they would spend the day eating, drinking, and laughing. It reminded me of my mom's group of friends, the Cookie Exchange Girls. Gabi and I even had a girls' night every two weeks. For girls' night, we'd make popcorn and hot chocolate, then watch a Spanish romantic comedy together on the couch.

Gabi often asked how my mom and Donna were doing. One time, I was FaceTiming my mom in the hospital because all the Big Kids were there, and Gabi got to say hello. My mom speaks fluent Spanish along with my siblings, so they were all chatting and laughing over FaceTime, which made me feel close to everyone. Gabi commented that my mom looked good even in her hospital gown in the hospital bed.

. . .

Only two weeks after I arrived in Buenos Aires, I was visiting a genocide memorial site with the program. Surrounded by so much death and sadness, I couldn't help but think about Donna.

As if reading my mind, my mom called me. "Hey Girlie, I just talked to Donna's nurse," she took a breath. "She said that today could be the day that she . . . goes to God." I sat down on the grass outside the museum and sobbed. Not caring who heard me or who saw me. Tears flowed out of my eyes like a river. I curled up and placed my arms around my knees.

"Aw . . . Girlie, I wish I were with you. I have a pillow on my lap and I'm patting it like I'd pat you on the back. Aww, Girlie."

I kept crying. I had no words left.

Hours later, once I was home from the field trip, my mom called me back. "I'm sitting outside Donna's house. She just passed away a couple of minutes ago." At this point my eyes were so dry and puffy, tears could barely fall. I just sat on my bed, crying softly. I asked to FaceTime just so I didn't feel alone, and my mom, Margaret, and I sat in silence together.

As if she knew, Gabi called me shortly after, *Cómo está tu madrina?* or "How is your godmother?"

I came home to Los Angeles for a week for Donna's funeral, to be there for Kate, to hug my Mama, and to help pack up Donna's house. It was so good to be surrounded by family during such a shitty time. My favorite part of this trip was sitting with my mom on the couch at night just cuddling and watching TV. We didn't have to talk. We had each other's company and that was enough.

. . .

After my week at home, I flew back to Buenos Aires to finish my research project and the academic program. Upon the culmination of the project, I headed north to Bolivia. I was supposed to meet a friend in La Paz, Bolivia, but at the border, they told me I needed a visa, and so I couldn't enter the country. Altitude-sick and frustrated, I sat down outside the border patrol office. I sat next to a Bolivian woman holding an umbrella to protect her from the sun. The officers told me I needed to go back to Chile and the next passenger bus wouldn't arrive for another seven hours. While most people may panic, my mom taught me to be smart and resourceful. She taught me to always be strong even when you feel like giving up.

I leaned over to the woman under the umbrella and asked in Spanish, "Excuse me, may I please borrow your phone to call someone on WhatsApp? I'm trying to find my way back to Chile and I need to call my mom."

"Yes, of course," she replied.

I entered in my mom's number. After only a couple rings, my mom picked up.

"Hello?"

"Hey Mama, it's Grace. Long story short, I'm stuck on the Bolivian border because I don't have a tourist visa, so I'm trying to get back to Chile. Can you call my friend in Bolivia and tell her I won't make it? I'm going to try and catch a ride with someone so I can get back to Arica, Chile, but I'll keep you updated."

While most mothers may have a heart attack in fear of their child being stuck on a border alone trying to hitchhike back, my mom simply said, "Ay, yai, yai. Okay, I'll call your friend. Be safe and keep me updated if you get into a car with someone. Do you need anything?"

"I'm okay, Mama. I'll keep you updated." I hung up, feeling better after talking to her.

After four hours of asking random cargo truck drivers to take me to Arica, someone finally said yes. The Bolivian man was middle-aged and had a dark brown beard. I grabbed my bags, which felt so heavy one might think I had rocks in them. Still feeling severely altitude sick, I climbed into the truck. Before starting the truck, I asked to borrow the truck driver's phone, and I sent a message on WhatsApp to my mom: "Hey Mama—it's Grace. Just got in a truck with a guy named René. I'm sharing my location with you and I should arrive in Arica in eight hours. Track his phone if anything happens." I learned later that during my hitchhiking adventure my mom was out to dinner with a friend. While my mom's friend panicked, my mom remained calm. My mom replied to her friend's concerns, "She's smart. She will figure it out like she always does."

Once buckled in, I took a breath. I prayed that I had not misplaced my trust.

CHAPTER 8

DON'T TAKE LIFE TOO SERIOUSLY

———

I survived hitchhiking across the Bolivian border and even became friends with the driver, René. We shared an interest in Spanish rock, especially the band Maná and listened to all of their albums during the ride. He even stopped at lookout points so I could take pictures. I arrived safely back in Arica, Chile, then spent the next two weeks traveling through Peru and Colombia, and I found my way back to Morocco to visit a friend.

I arrived at the Los Angeles Airport two days before Christmas. My mom and Arelly picked me up and took me to The Kettle, a restaurant that's open all night—perfect for late-night international arrivals. My mom leaned over the table to steal a French fry. Her renal diet limited her consumption of potatoes, but if she ate them from my plate, it didn't count, right? Once she finished chewing, she said, "So . . . what was the best part of your trip?"

The previous four months had been so jam-packed and fun-filled that it was hard to pull out one moment. I reflected on my time in Chile, Argentina, Peru, and Colombia, but my time in Morocco stood out to me. I got to visit my favorite country and see one of my favorite friends, Maddie, who was studying abroad there. I finally replied:

"I loved all the new people I met throughout the semester, but I was just so happy to be in Morocco at the end. While I love being social and everything, I was just so tired by the end that I had no energy left to meet new people. When I got to Morocco and saw Maddie, I literally cried because I was so happy to be with someone who knew me and who I didn't have to give the 'I'm Grace from America, studying abroad in South America' spiel. She and I went to a bakery every morning, then visited my Moroccan friends during the day, then we watched a romcom at night in the hostel. Oh! And I saw Ikbal, and I visited my host family. I visited Siham and Yousef; remember my Arabic teachers? OMG, Siham's children are so big now. I even got to see Mouad twice. Remember, the guy who translated for the workshops?"

Morocco is the most special place for me because my mom took me there on a work trip in 2015. I went back that summer to learn Arabic, then I went to visit friends again in 2017, and finally, I got to see everyone when I visited Maddie. It felt extra special that my mom knew the people I was talking about. As I told my story, my mom smiled, but her eyes drooped with sadness. She hadn't traveled abroad for more than two years, and traveling is our favorite thing to do together. I recognized the look in her eyes and reassured her, "In less than a month, you'll have a kidney, which means no more dialysis, and then you can even visit me in Georgetown as soon as April."

With that, her eyes sparkled, and she replied, "Oh! I can't wait!"

The two weeks I spent at home for Christmas and New Year's Eve were filled with fun. She'd become more accustomed to dialysis and her health seemed stable with the exception of the upcoming transplant. She loved when I took her to dialysis. She usually had two great friends who drove her to dialysis three days a week, but when I was in town, I would drive her and stay with her for all three hours. During dialysis I'd chat with her or work on my computer while she napped. One day at dialysis, we had a little too much fun. She had just gotten wireless earbuds, and I wanted to show her how to set them up.

"Okay, Mama, put this one in your right ear and tell me if you hear a sound."

She sat there in her dialysis chair draped in a blanket with a tube coming out of her chest, filtering her blood, while she fiddled with the ear bud, trying to get it to stay in her ear. "It's not working! I don't hear anything."

I got up and stood by her trying to figure out the AirPods when Kristina, one of the nurses, came over. "How's everything going, Pam?"

"Can't complain," she responded. "By the way, how's your daughter?"

"Actually, we just celebrated her birthday recently. She's five already." She pulled out her phone to show my mom a picture.

"She is cute! I love it," my mom said while holding the phone and zooming in to see her little face. As my mom handed the phone back, Kristina gestured to me and said, "So glad to see Grace is back from Morocco."

My mom replied, "Yes! I'm glad too. Finally, she's home, only for two weeks, but I'll take it. She goes back to Georgetown soon. Boohoo!"

Beep, beep, beep! When someone connected to a dialysis monitor moves too much, it beeps until a nurse comes and adjusts it.

"I gotta get that," Christina replied, "Talk to you both later."

My mom knew everyone at the dialysis center. Not only did she know their names, but she knew their stories too. She asked them about their kids, their partners, their dogs. She teased them. The staff would make fun of each other in a friendly way and my mom would pitch in with a witty comment.

Finally, I got the earbuds working, so I sat down in my chair and transformed into DJ Grace. Whenever my mom and I drove anywhere she would always ask me to DJ. I knew exactly what music she enjoyed and what music she hated. Even though she sat there, hooked up to a machine filtering her blood, the music kept her energetic. A combination of "Ain't No Mountain High Enough" and "You are the Sunshine of My Life" got my mom jamming. She and I had a silent disco dance party. We sang along to the song even though no one could hear the music. She started shimmying and bopping her head.

Beep, beep, beep!

She and I broke into a belly laugh. We laughed so hard my eyes began watering. Another nurse came over to see us in a laughing fit. I could barely get the words out through laughter, "She was . . . dancing . . . so much that she set off the monitor."

The nurses looked over with furrowed eyebrows, confused as to why we were giggling in the middle of a dialysis center. This moment reminded me of my mom's lesson to never take life too seriously. She'd say, "Why not have fun while you can?" Even if something bad happened, she'd be the first to laugh. Something I inherited from my mom was her clumsiness. But every time one of us fell, we broke into laughter instead of tears.

We had fun wherever we went—supermarkets, movie theaters, restaurants, and churches. On Christmas Eve, the night I returned to Los Angeles, I was jet-lagged, and she was tired. A man behind us sneezed during the service, which alone was not funny, but he followed the sneeze with a loud exclamation.

"God! That was loud!" His proclamation was so much louder than his sneeze that my mom and I simultaneously lost it. We had the giggles, and we couldn't stop. We tried to stop when the gospel reading began, but we couldn't and buried our faces into our chests.

We made it a goal in January to have the most fun week possible before I went back to school and before her surgery. I surprised her with tickets to a live recording of *The Voice*, and she took us out to dine in the dark; we were guided into a pitch-black room by a visually impaired waiter, and we proceeded to have a meal in the pitch black, which aims to heighten your other senses. We even went out to breakfast every day.

The most memorable activity we did together was an interview for an organization called StoryCorps. They take a van across the United States and invite people to do interviews, which they store in the national archive. My mom found out about it and wanted to do it with me so we'd have the interview as an archived memory.

We sat outside the van, waiting for our turn. We reviewed the questions we were planning to use to interview each other. "Mama, I think it's better if we ask questions on the spot so the answers are more natural!"

"I know you're good at improv, but I'd rather you pick three questions to ask me and tell me now so I have time to think about what my answers will be." While my mom and I are similar in many ways, she's always been more reflective before doing things, whereas I am more impulsive.

She might say, "Have you asked Arelly about doing nails on Sunday?" and by the time she'd finish the sentence, I would have already sent the text. She'd say "Jesus, Grace! Just listen. You don't have to do it right now." Being more thoughtful is probably the better thing to do, but it would be boring if we were the same person.

We stepped inside the recording room. "My name is Pam Rector. I am sixty-four years old; today's date is January 6, 2020." We talked about her decision to have a sperm donor baby, she asked me about what I want to be remembered for, and we finished the interview by singing the lullabies she sang to me as a child. I had no idea at the time how important this interview would become to me in the next few months.[1]

. . .

After a fun week with my mom, it was time to go back to school and reconnect with my friends after being apart for nine months. I arrived and was greeted by one of my best friends, Matt. He pulled up to the front gates in his mom's Honda minivan and I ran toward the car to give him a hug. I missed him so much. He is one of my friends who I can have deep conversations with because he knows me so well.

---

1   "Pam Rector and Grace Rector," StoryCorps Archive, StoryCorps, January 6, 2020.

He blasted some music for us along our journey to pick up my stuff from a family friend's house. We enjoyed each other's presence. When we arrived back at Georgetown to move my things into my apartment, my other good friends, Sania and Matthew (I know, two friends named Matthew!), waited for us. I saw Matthew and we stopped, bent our knees in sync, then ran toward each other and leaped into a hug. We greeted each other like this every time we saw each other on campus, and my heart swelled from being near my best friends again. Sania, Matthew, Matt, and I spent the next hour moving my things in, then rewarded ourselves with a cheese pizza. My mom taught me to celebrate every little thing, and that night we celebrated friendship.

The next morning, I got a text from one of my other best friends, Nico. "Yo! When can I see you?" My morning tiredness flew away in favor of the excited feeling in my stomach. I hadn't seen Nico in nine months. Thirty minutes later I heard a knock. I felt the excitement rise in my throat and I sprinted down the stairs. I opened the heavy apartment door and saw him on the other side. He stepped in and I threw my arms around him, sinking my face into his coat. I let go of him and beamed up at him.

He said, "Ah! I'm so happy to see you. Come here," and went in for another hug. I closed my eyes and smiled. I felt so delighted to be back with my community of friends. I loved traveling alone, but constantly creating community was exhausting. I was so grateful to have Nico and my other friends in DC with me.

Every morning I woke up smiling, knowing I had a community of people to support me. It made me think about how my mom had created family for us and how I was now making my own community at college. In addition to spending time with friends and taking classes, I also started a new job.

After my first day at work, I immediately called my mom on my walk to the metro. "Mama! I had the best first day at work. I have my own cubicle and everything. I met my boss, and he seems really great about the open-door policy. All the projects are right up my alley and I get to focus on storytelling to engage potential donors. I'm so happy!"

I didn't even stop for a breath. "*And* my classes are *all* amazing; literally, I love every single class. All the professors are emphasizing the importance of inquiry and questioning traditional interpretations of the subject. Like, my philosophy of education class—the professor is amazing and the students in it are awesome. I'm just really happy, Mama."

"Wow, Girlie! I'm so happy for you. It makes me so happy that you're enjoying your job and your classes so much. I'm so proud of you."

A smile radiated across my face. While I knew she was proud of me, she didn't say it often. I was on top of the world. I felt like such an adult—putting on a suit and heels every morning and taking the metro to work. I also loved my walks to the metro because I could call my mom every day while she was in dialysis. Work was great! Classes were great! And I had the most amazing friends around me!

Then came the week of my mom's transplant.

I had told my boss and professors beforehand that I'd miss a couple of days of school so I could be with my mom. I arrived in Los Angeles and immediately got dressed to go to church with my Mama. Her boss organized a prayer gathering after Mass to bless my mom and Anthony, her donor. She and I sat in the pews of the church. I put my arm around her, rubbing her back to comfort her. I knew she was excited for the transplant to be over, but I could also imagine she was nervous. After receiving communion, we had a couple minutes to pray independently. While I wanted to focus on praying for my Mama, Donna came to my mind and tears began to flow down my face. My mom heard me crying softly and held my hand.

Later in the Mass, I made eye contact with Anthony and motioned him over to sit with us. He crossed the aisle and joined us, then he placed his arm around my Mama. I looked over, smiling with yet more tears in my eyes. I couldn't vocalize my gratitude for Anthony and his decision to donate his kidney.

Following the Mass, fifteen members from my mom's LMU community, including Arelly and me, stood in a circle holding hands while Patrick, my mom's assistant director began, "Dear Lord, thank you for bringing us all together this evening to celebrate the love of the people in this room. We give thanks for Anthony's tremendous gift of life that he is giving to Pam this Tuesday. We pray, Lord, that the surgery goes well, and Pam comes away from it stronger and able to travel for years to come. Thank you for this community here to support Anthony and Pam. We give thanks Lord. Amen."

Tuesday morning, my mom came to wake me up at four o'clock. I loved the way she woke me up. She'd turn the lights on low then come sit on my bed. "Today's the day, Girlie. It's transplant day! Woohoo!" she said as she rubbed my back until I awoke. I sat up and gave her a hug.

"I'm so excited for you, Mama." I got up, got dressed, and piled into the car with Margaret and my mom. I offered to drive, but my mom said, "God knows how long it will be until I can drive again—I want to." I sat in the passenger's seat so

I could DJ. I looked over at my Mama as she drove and saw her eyes were filled with hope. I played songs about beauty and recovery: "It's a Beautiful Morning," "Every Little Thing Is Gonna Be Alright," and "I'm Coming Out!"

Upon our arrival, we even parked in parking spot number twenty-two. Two and twenty-two are our lucky numbers because I was born on February 22 at 6:22 a.m. Seeing our lucky number made us smile and reassured me that my Mama's surgery would go well.

I wasn't fearful at all, even as they took her into the operating room. I was just so excited for the life she'd have following the surgery. We sat with Anthony's family as we waited. His mom shared her feelings about the surgery. She leaned over and said, "I was so nervous and scared when Anthony told me he was donating his kidney. But when I told him not to do it, he said, 'I have to do it for Grace; Pam is all she has.' When he put it like that, I knew he had to do it. And I'm just so grateful he is so selfless and loving."

A tear fell down my face and I smiled. "We're so lucky to have Anthony in our life. He's not only giving my mom life, but he's also giving her hope."

She leaned over and held my hand, and we sat there as tears of gratitude continued to fall down my face.

After the kidney removal surgery, I got to go in and see Anthony. He looked so weak, but so happy. "Hi beautiful," he said weakly.

"Hi Anthony! How are you feeling?"

"I'm in a lot of pain, but I'll be okay." He, like my mom, is strong, so I was grateful he was honest about the pain with me. I stood there chatting with him trying to keep his mind off the pain.

"Do you need anything?"

"Yes, can you give me some water please?" I grabbed a cup of water from the side table and held it to his mouth as he sipped. While he looked weak in the hospital gown and ugly yellow socks, he was glowing. He had literally given the gift of life and he had every right to be proud.

"I love you so much, Anthony. Thank you." I smiled and held his hand lightly.

I made my way back to the waiting room and checked my phone for surgery updates. My godmother, Margaret, sat beside me the whole time. She even indulged me by listening to me read my class assignments out loud. Arelly was also there, making me laugh and teasing me. Ale and German also came to support my mom. Finally, around 8:00 p.m. they told us they finished the surgery and they moved her to the intensive care unit (ICU) to monitor her blood pressure since it had risen significantly during the operation.

I was so happy it had gone well and rushed to her room to see her. She was asleep, so I just sat there watching as the nurses changed things around her. I had dinner at the cafeteria downstairs with Margaret while my mom slept. When we came back to check on her, she was awake.

"Hiiii . . . Girlie," she said in slow slurred speech. My lip started trembling. The nurse reassured me she was on a lot of pain meds and she was really dehydrated, so the slurring was because her mouth was dry.

When she came to and had drunk several cups of water, I told her, "Hey, Mama, I pushed back my flight. I'm going to stay for a full week instead of leaving tomorrow." She smiled gently, which I took as an affirmative. I settled into the chair in her ICU room, prepared to spend the night. We didn't talk much, and I barely slept. Every time I closed my eyes, the fluorescent lights would turn on and several nurses would parade in to check my mom's vitals.

In the morning, she felt significantly better and begged the nurses to take her for a walk so she could start recovering quickly. Her nurse, Charlie, set her up on a walker. The three of us made our way slowly around the floor of the ICU. She pushed herself and the nurse was impressed with her quick recovery. I rubbed her back along the way and encouraged her, but she responded, "Don't touch me, I'm fine." I respected her independence and knew she hated to be talked down to. I walked alongside her as she cracked jokes with the nurse and asked him about his love life.

The next day in the ICU, we hung out and chatted. Finally, the nurses moved my mom to a bigger room in the main wing of the hospital after her blood pressure normalized. I asked her if she wanted me to stay. She quipped, "You know, I live by myself, you can leave me alone without worrying. Go home and get some sleep in a real bed."

I visited her every day with Margaret. We told stories, I did my homework when she slept, and we saw the Big Kids along with other visitors. One day, my mom handed me a stack of cards she received and said, "Hey Gracie Girl, can you tape these cards and photos on the wall? There should be more at home too if you could bring those." I asked her, "Do you just want it for decoration?" and she responded, "If each doctor and nurse who comes into my room sees the cards and photos on my wall, they'll see how many people love and depend on me. They'll be less likely to kill me; they'll work harder to keep me alive." She joked, but there was also some truth in her words. She had the superpower of blending humor into the seriousness of life.

On my last day in Los Angeles, she had still not been approved to leave the hospital. I arrived in the morning. "Hey Mama! How are you doing?"

"I'm in a shit ton of pain," she replied.

"Aw, Mama, I'm so sorry, do you need anything?" My mom's pain tolerance was higher than anyone else I knew, so if she said she was in pain, it was *bad*.

"I'm just going to lie here and try to rest."

I set up my school readings on her side table and pulled up a chair. She laid there in bed, eyes squeezed tightly in pain. I felt powerless. I talked to her whenever she felt like it. From 9:00 a.m. until 11:00 p.m. I sat in the chair beside her, reading books and writing papers, checking in on her when she was awake. When it was time to head home to pack for my flight back to DC, I said, "Hey Mama, it's getting late. I think I'm going to go home."

"Okay, Girlie." She paused and strained to turn my way with a sad look on her face, "I'm sorry I was no fun today."

"Don't worry at all, Mama. I'm happy to be here for company even if you can't chat."

"Didn't you bring the party dresses?" While my mom was in the hospital, she, Margaret, and I planned my twenty-first birthday party that Nico was helping me host in DC. We decided on The Roaring '20s for the theme, so I'd ordered a couple of 1920s flapper dresses for potential birthday girl outfits.

"I did bring them."

"How about you try them on anyway; that could be fun." She really tried hard to be a fun mom. When I was thirteen years old, I told her she wasn't fun because all we did together were errands and serious stuff, and that really stuck with her.

I know it hurt her feelings, but since I told her that, she put extra effort into doing fun things with me.

I admired her for trying to make it fun despite the pain she was going through. I tried on the first dress in front of her bed. It clung to my stomach and was a deep blue color. The embroidered pattern on the front swelled around my hips. "Okay! Dress number one," I announced.

She opened her eyes briefly and responded weakly, "Oh no! That's unflattering! It's tight in the wrong spots." Then she shut her eyes again. She is my chief critic, so finding clothes she likes is close to impossible. But her critiques were always valid, so I always listened.

I put on another dress. This one was bright red and covered in sparkles with tassels dangling off the bottom. "What about this one, Mama?"

Again, she strained to open her eyes. "Not that one! Unless you want to look like you belong on *Dancing with the Stars* in a bad costume."

I tried on a dark red dress with a more subtle design embroidered in white string. "How's this, Mom?"

"That one is okay. The waist fits you better and I like the color." Sold!

"Okay! I'll wear this one," I answered, content she liked one of them.

I stuffed all the dresses into my bag. I walked over and kissed her forehead, then, I made my way back to DC.

. . .

Back at Georgetown, I got updates from my mom. She told me her health soon improved, and the hospital discharged her. Over the next two weeks, Margaret took care of her, and my mom continued to check on me. Since she couldn't work during recovery, she did research for me on fun things to do in DC.

She told me about Restaurant Week in DC, a week in which local restaurants have several-course meals for a lower price. She sent me a gift card and suggested I take my friends to a participating restaurant that I loved, Jaleo. I followed her advice and went to dinner at Jaleo with my friends Tommy, Nico, Sania, and Yuri.

I sat there between Yuri and Sania, all three of us watching Tommy and Nico crack each other up. We wore smiles throughout the entirety of the meal. Each new course arrived, making us "mmm" in unison. Once we finished all four courses, we gathered our things and walked to the Capitol to take photos. Sania and I hugged each other tightly while Nico took our picture.

"Ooh! I wanna be in one," Nico shouted. He and I posed dramatically back-to-back while holding back giggles. Then Nico called Tommy over and I took a picture of the two goofballs posing. I love my friends. I found myself being more present and grateful for everything around me instead of focusing on the future.

. . .

One day after class, an attractive classmate of mine approached me. His good looks and charm made me nervous.

"Hey Grace, would you want to grab coffee sometime? My treat," he offered.

I looked back with a smile. "Um . . . that would be nice. Maybe next weekend?" I suggested.

"Great!" He responded excitedly. "I'll see you next weekend then." I'd never been properly asked out on a date, so his proposal was exciting to me. Not only did I love my friends and my classes, but I also had the prospect of going on a date with a nice guy. I walked home from class to find that my friend, Nico, was waiting for me.

"Hi!" he exclaimed.

"Hey! How are you doing?" I said while opening the door to my apartment.

"I have news," He said mysteriously. "I'm running for student body president!"

"OMG, seriously? That's so exciting! I'll help with flyers or whatever you need."

"Do you want to be my chief of staff if I win?" Naturally, I agreed.

A month later he, his running mate, the rest of the campaign team, and I stood in his apartment anxiously awaiting the call from the election commission with the results of the election. Nico's phone buzzed. We turned off the music. He didn't put the phone on speaker, but he smiled. We waited.

"Okay, thank you so much," he replied.

We waited.

"We won!"

The music blasted again; everyone's faces were filled with smiles. Nico and his running mate embraced; I made a beeline for Nico and gave him a jumping hug. *We did it!*

One could say I was the happiest I'd ever been in my life: I had a job I loved, I adored all of my classes, I was in the student government, and my mom was proud of me. However, good things don't always last.

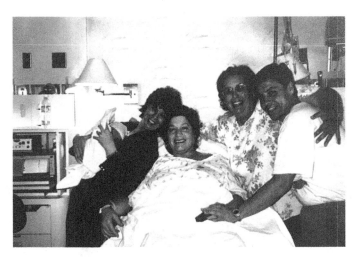

The day I was born

Shhh . . . no one can know the secret of the Rector Girls

Snuggle buggles with Mama (2003)

Snuggle buggles with Mama (2019)

Mother Daughter Luncheon

My extended family supporting me in my show

It's always a party at my mom's house

Finding the joy in life with my mama

The Big Kids at my high school graduation

My mom is now an angel

AFTER

CHAPTER 9

TAKE A DEEP BREATH

———

I walked around the Apple store searching for an Apple Watch for my mom. In a conversation we'd previously had, I said, "Mom—I would feel more comfortable if you had a life alert necklace or watch that called 911 if you fell. I just don't like thinking of you living by yourself, God forbid anything happens." That week she'd been readmitted to the hospital because she was experiencing pain again, three weeks following the transplant.

"Gracie, I'm fine. I'll be fine, but if it makes you more comfortable, I will get a watch."

I walked along the display cases looking for the words *fall detection*. The watches were expensive, but my mom's health was priceless. "Hello, miss, can I help you?"

"Hi, I'm looking for a watch that has fall detection. It's for my mom."

"I'd be happy to show you some models." He directed me to a wooden table with several watches laid out. "The cheapest watch we have with fall detection is $400."

Wow. That is a lot of money, I thought to myself. Maybe the Big Kids would help me pay for it. I thanked the salesclerk and made my way out of the store. I rented an electric scooter and started my journey back to the hotel where I was staffing a Model UN conference for the weekend. On my way back, I saw a donut shop, so I stopped to buy donuts for the staff members in my committee.

I served as the chair of the Arab League for the Model UN conference, leading other freshmen staff members. Georgetown hosts an annual conference for high school students who come from around the world. On the second day of the conference, I banged the gavel and invited the next speaker to come up and give the speech on behalf of their country. I took notes on my notepad while the student spoke. I glanced at my phone to check the time and saw eight missed calls. I saw three missed calls from Margaret, two missed calls from Arelly, one missed call from German, and two missed calls from unknown numbers. I felt a knot in the pit of my stomach, but I waited until the speaker finished to excuse myself. I cleared my throat, "By the power vested in me, I pass the gavel to the vice chair."

I left the room and called Arelly back. "What's going on Arelly?"

"Call Margaret!" she said urgently.

"Okay." Her curt response spurred the knot to rise to my chest.

I dialed Margaret's number tentatively, scared of what awaited me on the other end. "Hello?"

"Hi, Gracie," she responded with a weak and shaking voice.

"What happened?"

"Your mom . . ." she paused. "She had a heart attack this morning."

"What?" My heart stopped. I stepped out of the hallway and into a small room. My eyes filled with tears. Then all of a sudden, my phone rang, and an unknown number appeared. "Someone's calling me, Margaret."

"Answer it. It might be her doctor"

I picked up. "Hello? Grace? This is Dr. Kim. Your mom's kidney doctor."

"What's going on? Is she okay?"

She paused "We don't know what happened. I'm so sorry . . ." Her voice began to waver. "I've never seen anything like this. She was fine last night."

I began to sob. I could no longer stand. I buckled over and bent my knees, trying to get air.

"The team tried to resuscitate her for thirty minutes to no success, so they took her into surgery and now she's in a medically induced coma."

I still couldn't breathe. My sobs echoed through the phone. "I . . ."

Dr. Kim jumped in, "Grace, I am so sorry." I could hear a sniffle on the other end.

". . . Just do everything you can. Please . . . she's everything to me. She's all I have. Please," I sobbed.

"Oh, Grace. We will try everything. Just get here as soon as possible."

I called Margaret in a voice wavering uncontrollably, "I'm coming. Please help me get a ticket."

I called Abby, my best friend from Bosnia, and she immediately answered. "Hey babe, what's up?"

I shriek-cried into the phone, "I . . . my . . . my mom had a . . . heart attack."

"Oh honey—oh no." I filled her silence with sobs. "Can I say a prayer?"

"Yes, please."

"Dear Lord Jesus, please send your strength and healing to Pam right now. She needs your love, Lord, she needs your strength. Please help her recover. Grace needs her."

. . .

Everything after was a blur. I called my friend, Tommy, in tears. Barely getting out the words, I muttered, "Please . . . meet me at the front gates." I dragged my feet as I walked outside of the hotel. I wore only a shirt and a skirt, but even though it was 30° F, I couldn't feel anything. My Uber pulled up. I climbed in without a word and dropped my head into my hands. During the fifteen-minute ride I said nothing; I just sat in the back, crying. We stopped and I lugged my body out of the car. Barely managing to stand, I focused my eyes, blurry from tears, on the front gates. Tommy patiently stood there with a concerned look on his face. I made my way toward him. My entire face drooped, and I tightly wrapped my arms around me as if I'd fall apart if I let go. As I got closer to him, I sped up my walk until I ran straight into his arms. He held me tightly as my whole body shook from my sobs. I buried my face into his jacket and held on for a long time, not caring who saw me or what he was thinking.

I let go. He saw me shivering, even though my brain didn't know it was cold. He placed his jacket around my shoulders. My body seemed to weigh a million pounds. Walking took so much energy. I felt so unstable that if he weren't there to hold me upright, I'd fall right over. He put his arm around me, kept me steady, and walked me to his room. He pulled out a chair and sat me down. I could barely speak, only cry. "My mom . . ." I couldn't continue; sobs consumed me. "She had a heart attack."

He sat beside me, rubbing my back. There was nothing he could say to make it better. I hunched over in the chair, breathing deeply. A skill my mom taught me to do when I get overwhelmed. *It's okay. People recover from heart attacks all the time. It's just a medically induced coma. They could take her off and she'll be fine.* I thought. *But what if she's not... Oh my god.* The thought sent me into another round of sobs. *There's no life without Mama. She's my everything. She was supposed to be better. What the hell happened? I don't deserve this. I was happy. My mom was hopeful. Why the hell would God do this to me?*

Tommy's hand entered my periphery, clutching a bottle of water. "Want some water?" he asked. I looked up at him and joked amidst the sobs, "Gotta replenish my tears, don't I?" He gave a sad smile. Once my wracking sobs slowed, he took me to get some food, then took me home to pack a suitcase.

. . .

The five-hour flight home was the longest flight I've ever been on. I sat in my seat shifting every two seconds. I reached up to turn on the air because my jacket felt like it was burning my skin. But once the cold air came streaming out, I began to shiver. I turned it off, and then took out my phone. I shuffled my music and it started with an upbeat song. The energy and happiness in the song made me grind my teeth in anger. How dare anyone be happy when my Mama was not okay! I changed it to a sad song, only to find myself sobbing again. I changed it back to a happy song and tensed my body, then changed to a sad song and cried more. So, I ripped off my headphones and put my phone in the pocket in front of me. I thought to myself, *Jesus! How has it only been fifteen minutes since we took off? It feels like it's been two hours, and I still have five hours left. How am I going to survive this? Maybe I should sleep! That way I don't have to think about my Mama.*

I closed my eyes and nestled into the airplane seat, but behind my closed eyes were nightmares. My head filled with the worst-case scenarios that could happen to my mom and tears fell from behind my eyelids. I gave up on sleep and looked out the window, counting down the minutes until I was with my Mama.

I came into the ICU waiting room with Margaret and saw the Big Kids and Liz: Ale, Arelly, German, and Jorge. I melted into each and every one of them as waterfalls of tears spilled out of my eyes. I let them hug me until my eyes were bloodshot and empty. Then the nurse came and asked if I wanted to see my Mama. I entered her room and saw her lying there, a plastic tube coming out of her mouth and so many different colored cords crossing her body. Her eyes were closed, and she looked like she was taking a nap. Her chest rose and fell. There was a little crackle in her exhale like she did when she would fall asleep on the couch while we were watching a TV show. I reached out to touch her, but the nurse stopped me, "I'm sorry but you shouldn't touch her. She's sensitive right now and any touch could put her in shock." A tear rolled down my cheek. I was so sad and angry and confused and upset. "There will be no change for your mom until tomorrow, so you're welcome to stay or go home," the nurse said. I looked over to Margaret who was by my side. "Aw Grace, you look tired." Margaret observed. My eyes glowed red from all the tears that had emptied me throughout the day. I nodded and Margaret took me home.

The next morning, I woke up in bed with Margaret and gently cuddled into her arms, missing my Mama every single second. She held me closely and cried softly. The bed was large and soft and felt like a big hug; Margaret's embrace was comforting, but still I needed my Mama. I got up and went into the shower. As soon as the water started streaming over my body, something broke inside of me. My body filled with wracking sobs. A scream, one I've never heard before, escaped from my throat. It was a deep guttural groan that encapsulated how it feels to be without your mama. I laid down in the tub, letting water drown around my body. I no longer knew what was tears and what was bath water. I let another scream come from me underwater as I watched the bubbles float up to the surface. Tempted to stay down a little longer, I held my breath.

My lungs grew tired, and I couldn't hold my breath any longer. I burst through the surface of the water feeling empty—no more tears could come.

Margaret and I exited the elevator doors on my mom's floor, the intensive care unit. I was greeted by the tired and solemn faces of Ale, German, Jorge, Liz, and Arelly. Before I could reach them, a nurse blocked my path. "Excuse me. Are you Grace Rector?"

I hesitated, "Yes . . ."

"I need you to come with me to make some decisions about your mom."

She had just said the worst sentence I could ever imagine in such a nonchalant way.

I melted into the floor, releasing a terrible groan out of my soul. Margaret held me, which only made me cry more. I felt her arms wrapped around me, then I felt Arelly's arms replace hers, followed by Ale, then Liz, then German, then Jorge. I followed the nurse like a zombie—feeling nothing, thinking nothing, just feeling dead inside.

If I had to make decisions about my mom, that meant she was not okay. It hit me. *I don't think she's going to be okay. My mom, my world, may not come home with me ever again. It has always just been me and her, but now it could just be me.*

I entered a dark and ugly conference room the size of a closet with Margaret by my side. The walls were this terrible dark brown color that made you feel like you were underground. The ugly white floors were stained with the footsteps of family members who had previously come to hear terrible news about their loved ones. The light was dim although it felt hot. The shitty wooden table I sat at made me clench my fists. The bulky plastic blue chairs were the same as those I sat in during middle school. Outside the tiny conference room, the loud beeping of monitors and muffled conversations between nurses and doctors echoed. I should have felt safer in this room but being at that little table in the plastic chairs with the hot lighting made me seethe with anger.

I looked up at a doctor across from me who I'd never seen before. My mom's doctor was out of town, and I had no inclination to trust this guy with my mom's life. With my hands still clenched, Margaret placed a light hand over my fists. I let them soften a bit and let one hand slip away to hold her hand. In that moment my eyes glazed over, words flowed out of the doctor's mouth, and Margaret took notes. I heard none of it. I didn't gain awareness until he uttered two words, "brain death." My eyes widened. I blinked. I breathed. My body went into shock. Tears quietly fell down my cheek, but I had no sobs left in my body.

The doctor went on, but Margaret stopped him, "Can you pause for a moment so we can take that in?"

Tears streamed down her face and she continued to rub my hand. I just blinked.

The doctor took a breath, "She suffered too much damage during the attempts to resuscitate her." The doctor continued, "We can do one more test to confirm that there's no chance, but it may take a while. She's currently on an ECMO machine that beats her heart and forces her to breathe. We're still giving her blood transfusions. She's not in any pain. We can take her off the machine or leave her on it for another twenty-four hours. What measures do you want us to take?"

I took a deep breath. I felt my mom's spirit take on mine. I replied, "We don't need the test. She wouldn't want to waste blood that could save someone else's life, so stop giving her blood. She would love to be a donor to someone else, so please see if you can donate her skin or any organs." I looked at Margaret whose eyes sparkled with tears. She seemed proud of me for maturely handling this decision. "I think we should take her off the machine. Even if she was miraculously able to still be alive, brain death would not allow her to live a full life—and she would hate that. What do you think?"

Margaret nodded. "You're right."

I turned back to the doctor. "Okay, we can take her off the machine. But can we have time with her before you do?"

"Of course," he replied.

"It would be wonderful if we could have a chaplain come to bless her. Peggy, the Catholic chaplain would be best because she did reiki on my mom once. But if she's not available, I'd love a nun or priest."

"I'll check for you. Would you like me to send your family back?"

I nodded.

He exited the ugly room, and Margaret sat there holding me in her arms while I leaned into her feeling like an empty vessel. I felt numb. Even the ugly room didn't feel so ugly because nothing seemed to matter anymore.

The door opened, and the Big Kids and Liz came in. I looked at the ground studying each groove in the floor. After seconds of silence that felt like hours, I looked up but not into to anyone's eyes—as that would break me further. I breathed and heard some whimpers from my brothers and sisters.

"Mom . . ." my voice broke. "She experienced brain death after thirty minutes of CPR." I heard Ale holding in a sob. "So, I decided we should take her off the ECMO," I paused. "Mom's gone." A wail sounded out and echoed off the walls, but I had no idea who it came from. German came to me and leaned down, wrapping me in a hug that made me feel safe for a while. A sob came out of me that got worse as I hugged each of the Big Kids. We took turns holding one another and crying for the mom we had all lost.

Liz held me close and whispered to me, "I'm so sorry, Gracie."

We stood around my mom's hospital bed sharing our favorite memories with her out loud. I pulled up a chair to my mom holding her hand and resting my head on her chest. I tried lying next to her but there were too many cords and machines in the way.

German looked at mom and said, "I love how you blamed me for teaching Gracie to curse even though you cursed way more than me." We all laughed with tears in our eyes.

Ale went next, "Thank you Mom . . . for teaching me how to be a good mom to Maya. I c . . ." she paused to suck in a tear, "I couldn't do it without you. She's amazing thanks to you, Mom." She cried, and Arelly reached out to hold her hand.

Margaret followed, "I love how you always make the person you're talking to feel like the most important person in the world. I am *so* lucky you chose me to be your best friend in the world."

I held in my sobs so I could say, "I love how you always answer my calls even if it's 2 a.m. or 6 a.m." The Big Kids laughed. ". . . I'm just gonna miss you so much Mama." I let out a wave of new tears.

"Should we say a prayer?" Margaret asked. "Sí." Ale replied. Margaret and I recited the Our Father prayer in English while the Big Kids began, "Nuestro Padre, que está en el cielo. . . " I held mom's hand and German's hand. He connected hands with Jorge and so on until our circle with Mom was completed when Margaret took Mom's hand in hers. I closed my eyes and felt energy flowing through our hands. I smiled thinking of how happy mom would be to have all of us together in the same room.

A rabbi entered the room. "Hello, I'm Lynn. There were no Catholic chaplains, but I'm available if you want me." We all smiled because my mom could not care less what religion someone practiced; she was inclusive that way.

The drive home was somber until I realized it. "OMG," I said out loud. "I told Mom a long time ago that I wanted to get a tattoo of our family heart, and Mom said, 'Yeah, not while I'm alive you won't!'"

The Big Kids laughed. I paused.

"I have to get the tattoo," I said in a surprised tone of voice. I had never actually planned on getting it. "I want to get one too," Ale exclaimed. I laughed. "Arelly! You should get one too," I joked.

"Yeah, maybe" She replied in a serious tone. We all smiled at the thought of Mom shaking her head saying, "Tattoos are stupid." I turned up the music because I knew mom wouldn't want us to be sad; she'd want us to enjoy our time together.

My mom had a heart attack on Valentine's Day. I think her heart gave out because she'd given so much love to those around her that she ran out of love to give. She gave more to others by the time she was sixty-four than most people give out in their life. As Father Greg Boyle, a friend of my mom's, said, "Pam brings love to places that haven't seen love."

CHAPTER 10

CELEBRATE EVERYTHING

———

The days that followed my Mama's death felt like years.

I was grateful to have my family around. Arelly and Margaret stayed at my house, and Ale and Liz spent as much time at Mom's house as they could. We cleaned every drawer, cupboard, and closet. We broke bread together and prayed for my mom at every meal. Family friends brought food, photos, and their company. I found old home videos that my mom recorded. Her voice narrating videos of me as a baby sent shivers down my spine.

One night, Ale, Arelly, Margaret, Liz, and I sat in the living room surrounding the TV to listen to the StoryCorps interview that my mom and I had done only a month earlier. We laughed in awe of how Mom seemed to plan everything. She'd rewritten her will, cleaned the garage with the Big Kids, done the interview with me, and talked to me about passwords and financials only a month before she passed. I looked around at the incredible women I have in my family. I smiled and thought of my mom's obsession with gratitude despite all the shit in the world, including her tumultuous health and Donna's death. She found gratitude so crucial that she created a license plate that reads "GGGR8FL." For now, the Rector Girls were apart; I needed to learn how to be grateful despite the feeling that the world was a terrible, hostile place.

· · ·

My Mama always reminded me to not take life too seriously and to celebrate everything. My birthday came exactly one week after she died, and I did not feel like celebrating at all. But Margaret, the best godmother of all time, pushed back. She exclaimed, "Your mom would have celebrated you *so* hard. It's your twenty-first!" I paused and considered whether she was right. "Let's make a list," Margaret said with a smile. I looked back with a smirk. She and I always joke that I got my organizational skills from her because I also love lists, whereas my mom was pretty disorganized.

The day before my twenty-first birthday, my friend Nico arrived in Los Angeles. He expected his trip to Los Angeles would be somber and he'd have to focus on comforting me. However, my mom would want us to make my birthday weekend as fun as possible, even though my mom's funeral was on Monday.

I decided to put on my tourist hat the first day Nico arrived. I took him to downtown Los Angeles to eat at Grand Central Market, then we walked to the Art District as I pointed out landmarks along the way. Despite it being the worst week of my life, I smiled the whole time I was with Nico. He has a way of making everything fun. When we stopped for In-N-Out burgers on our way home, Nico fed me fries as

I drove. However, when you're driving seventy miles per hour on the freeway, it's a bad idea. He reached toward me with a ketchup-loaded fry. As the fry neared my lips, the wind from the window whipped my hair and tangled the ketchup into my hair. He paused and looked at me with surprise. Then I realized what happened and cracked up. He followed suit and we laughed for a long time. Laughing with him was so refreshing because crying all the time was exhausting.

At 11:59 p.m. on February 21, Nico, Arelly, Liz, Margaret, Pat (Margaret's husband), Mark (my godfather), Bryan (Mark's partner), and I gathered around the fire in my backyard. When a minute passed, and it was officially February 22, Margaret and Mark emerged with a lemon Bundt cake topped with candles. "Happy birthday to you!" they sang. My eyes sparkled with both joy and sadness because I wasn't used to anyone presenting the cake other than my Mama. We sat around the fire laughing as Nico, Pat, and Mark discussed old movies. We even played chubby bunny, where you try to stuff as many marshmallows as possible into your mouth at once. It seems stupid but doing something so silly when the world feels so serious was so nice. I smiled softly, "I'm so grateful to have you all in my life."

The following morning, I woke up and I was twenty-one! I came out to the dining room to see that Margaret had placed streamers across the ceiling, taped balloons on the walls, hung a giant "Hooray!" sign above the couch, and even slipped a cover over a chair that read "Birthday girl!" I felt like a child again. Being a kid again was amazing because losing my mom made me feel like I had gained ten years of life. My high school best friend, Grace, came over, and her sweet parents made breakfast for my birthday squad: Margaret's family, the Big Kids, Grace, and Nico. We sat around Mom's table laughing and eating pancakes. Margaret's daughter brought over ingredients for mimosas—the perfect ingredient for a twenty-first birthday breakfast!

. . .

Next on the agenda was tattoos!

"Hello? We're at the tattoo shop, but no one is here," Ale said into the phone.

"I'll be there soon," said Alex, the man who would be giving Arelly, Ale, Megan (Margaret's daughter), and I our tattoos!

She hung up and we all squirmed in excitement. I turned around from my passenger's seat and looked at everyone in the minivan. Margaret's husband, Pat, had been thoughtful enough to rent a minivan for the week so everyone could travel together for my birthday. It reminded me of my mom's old minivan. It's funny that a single mom with one daughter had a minivan, but my mom said she always got a big car so she could drive lots of people around, whether it be the Big Kids, my Girl Scout troop, or students from her university.

Megan exclaimed, "I can't believe we're doing this!"

"I know. I never thought I'd get a tattoo," I replied.

Ale laughed. "I already have tattoos. I'm a pro."

"Is it gonna hurt?" Arelly asked with a nervous squirm. "Never mind, it's gonna hurt."

Alex opened up the shop and we followed in after him. We were all ready to go after signing consent forms, then we saw Margaret signing a consent form. "Wait. Margaret, are you? Are you getting a tattoo?" I shouted.

Margaret shyly replied, "When I was writing my eulogy and I mentioned the family heart, I realized I had to get it."

She held up the drawing, "See? Around the heart are six lines, the six loves of her life: (1) Grace, (2) Arelly, (3) Ale, (4) German, (5) Jorge, and (6) Liz."

I smiled in response, "I love that!"

"Who is up first?" Alex asked.

Everyone looked at me. "It is *your* birthday, Gracie," Ale said with a giggle.

I swallowed hard. I painted a huge smile on my face in excitement, but I wondered, *what if it hurts really bad? What if he messes up?*

I sat down in the padded black chair with a folding chair pulled up to the side. Margaret sat in the chair on the side, holding my right hand while the tattoo artist, Alex, took my left. He placed an alcohol wipe on my wrist, and I gasped. I was so nervous the cold alcohol wipe startled me. The needle came down on my arm. If I didn't look, it seemed like someone was poking me with a toothpick over and over again. It didn't feel great, but I didn't mind because I looked at Liz's grinning face behind the camera she was recording with. I saw Arelly laughing and videotaping me on Snapchat. There was Ale just smiling as she saw her baby sister get a tattoo. The prickly feeling continued, and I breathed deeply as my mom taught me. Alex placed a clear wrap over it and said, "Done!" I finally exhaled. "It wasn't bad at all," I shared proudly.

Next was Megan, so Margaret stayed to hold her daughter's hand. Then it was Arelly, and I held her hand. The song "Hotel California" came on and we all burst out singing together and laughing at the fact that we were having a karaoke party in a tattoo parlor. Next was Ale, who took it like a pro. Last was Margaret. Megan sat beside her, watching her mom get a tattoo. "What a hoot!" my mom would say. Or she'd say, "Margaret got a fucking tattoo? Who would have thought?" We left the shop proudly showing off our new ink!

Later that night my best friend, Rimsha, who I'd met in Morocco four years earlier, arrived at my house. To have Nico and Rimsha with me was the greatest gift I could ask for. As soon as she arrived, I excitedly pulled her by the hand to get ready with me in the bathroom.

Once all dolled up, we drove to my favorite restaurant in the world: The Bazaar. I sat between my friends as we devoured each delicious tapa that arrived at the table. I ordered my first alcoholic drink and was blown away by the price of a cocktail. Margaret noticed my dilemma and reminded me that my mom would say, "Life is too fucking short! Enjoy it."

I missed my mom, but I was so happy and grateful to have so many people around who love me so much. We ate course after course and got more and more full. From caviar to Caprese salad to Philly cheesesteak, we tried it all. The older folks dropped Rimsha, Nico, Grace, and me off at a bar in West Hollywood to use twenty-one-plus benefits to the max. But we were *so* full. Inside the first bar we went to, even looking at alcohol made me feel sick because we'd eaten so much good food at the restaurant. "I can't! I'm too full!" I pleaded.

"I have an idea. Let's go dancing. Burn off that food," Rimsha exclaimed. Nico started pulling his drunk dance moves and I laughed.

"Let's go!" I exclaimed as I followed Rimsha down the street.

I wobbled on my uncomfortable heels and Grace smiled in her tennis shoes. The streets were empty, but music blared from surrounding clubs and young drunk people stumbled down the streets. Then I heard a club playing "Jessie's Girl."

"OMG guys! We have to go here," I said excitedly. Nico led us into the bar, and we discovered a DJ playing music for an empty dance floor. It was *perfect!* A private club for ourselves. We danced outrageously. Our dopey smiles were glued to our faces. I looked over at Rimsha. She was gliding all over the dance floor and would occasionally grab me to dance with her.

Being near her made me forget about the pain in the world. I hadn't seen her in over a year since I'd visited her in Chicago. You know how there are some people you meet randomly and they're so perfect for you that you think to yourself, "This has to be fate?" Rimsha is one of those people. I've never met someone who gets me as she does. She can read my mind, she knows when to be crazy with me and when to chill; she's always down for an adventure, and she also loves talking to strangers. I was so glad she and my other friends could spend my birthday with me. We made our way home. Once back in my mom's house, Rimsha and Nico hugged me tight in anticipation of the hardest day of my life: my Mama's funeral.

. . .

I walked down the aisle following the Big Kids. Although my immediate family was just my mom and me, the church was packed. I looked to my right to see a sea of people dressed in black. Their faces were streaked with tears although the service had not even begun. I caught the eyes of a former coworker of my mom's. His eyes were covered in sadness and pity for me: the girl who lost her single mom at twenty years old. I continued walking slowly toward the altar but could not bear the thousands of pairs of eyes focused on me. For the first time in my life, I put my head down instead of connecting with those around me. I wanted to turn around and run out of the church because I didn't want to be there. I didn't want this to be happening. But that wouldn't change my reality.

I kept my head down as tears poured down my cheeks. I clenched on tighter to the box in my hand. The delicate box held an even more delicate, colorful bracelet my mom had worn every day since I had given it to her. Now it was mine to wear. Now her community was mine to take care of.

Once I made my way to the *ofrenda* that we had set under her photo, I placed the box with her bracelet on the table. When I turned around, Donna's daughter—my god-sister Kate, embraced me. Kate rarely shows her emotions, so it was meaningful to me when she reached up and told me, "Now we just have each other, Gracie. Our moms left us for each other." I then reached to my left where I found my other sister's hand. As Arelly held my hand, the tattoos on the insides of our wrists perfectly aligned together.

Margaret and my mom's colleague, Patrick, both gave beautiful eulogies, then Arelly nudged me. It was my time to speak. I walked up to the podium silently and slowly. Usually a fan of the spotlight, this time I felt shy and nervous. I partly felt this way because I had decided to sing Josh Groban's "You Raise Me Up" at my mom's funeral, but also because there were so many people. I looked out into the sea of black clothing and saw individuals who had known my mom for two years and others who had known her for forty years. I saw her friends who had flown in from Cambodia just to celebrate her life. I saw the students who had worked in her office at

LMU ten years ago. I saw her coworkers. I saw individuals who called my mom Ms. Rector when she was a counselor at Lennox Middle School. I saw my friends from the local community theater who I hadn't seen in ten years. I saw my fifth-grade teachers and first-grade teacher. I saw my mom's bosses. I saw Jesuit priests who loved her. I saw current LMU students who knew her. I saw a staff member from my university who had flown from Washington, DC to be there. I saw my two best friends from New York and Kentucky sitting in the second row with a look full of love and support.

I struggled to open my mouth and start my song.

My mom raised me to be strong, but also to love wholeheartedly. I looked out again at all the people there who loved my mom. The music began and I swallowed hard. The first note that came out of my mouth sounded off. I stopped. I looked back at the pianist with a frightened look. He gestured with his hands to remind me to breathe. The music started again and this time I closed my eyes. I began to sing. It sounded right. I focused on the back wall, too afraid to make eye contact. As I continued to sing, I noticed that looks of pity and sorrow turned into soft smiles with tears falling down their faces. The more than eight hundred individuals who came to my mom's funeral were just a portion of the community she was a part of and a portion of the people in the world she had touched. The big irony is that she would have loved to be in that room catching up with everyone about everything; however, I'm sure she was watching over us and watching us connect. She continues to bring people together even after her death.

. . .

The unfortunate thing about grief is that most people are super present for the funeral and the two weeks after the death of your loved one. However, this often slowly fades away. My best friends had to go back to school, fewer people came by the house, Margaret went home to Seattle, and the Big Kids had to go back to work.

I felt hopeless; however, after moping around for weeks, I thought about my Mama. She wouldn't want her death to defeat me and make me a miserable person. I thought about the things she loved. Maybe by doing what she loved I might be happier and feel less empty. Her legacy was to love people who needed the most love.

I decided to be strong and persevere through the pain just like my mom did throughout the roller coaster of her health. Being strong doesn't mean I can't cry; it means to carry the loss in my heart but continue to get things done.

Years ago, my mom and I sat on the couch "snuggle buggling." While I cried in her arms, she told me, "The Rector Girls don't have time to mope around! We cry it out and hard, then we move on because we've got shit to do."

My mom loved learning, traveling, and meeting people. I planned to go to Cambodia for an educational program for spring break 2020, but it was canceled due to COVID-19. I instead went to Bosnia so I could be with a dear friend of mine, Abby. She, like Nico, also didn't know my mom, which helped to take my mind off the grief for a little bit. I didn't have to worry whether they were grieving. I landed in Sarajevo and a huge smile took over my face. My mind filled with good memories of when I resided in Bosnia less than a year ago. On our first day, Abby and I went to our favorite coffee shop, bumped into my ex-coworkers, ate at my favorite restaurant, and climbed to the best lookout spot in the city to watch the sunset.

Unfortunately, my trip got cut short. Abby and I sat at a restaurant for dinner, and she looked down at her phone. "OMG!" She exclaimed. "They just declared a state of emergency because of the Coronavirus." Then she looked up from her phone to my face with a frown. She knew that meant I had to go home before it was too late.

We made it to her apartment at 11:00 p.m. I booked a flight for five o'clock the next morning. I held Abby tightly in my arms before crawling into the back of the taxi, not knowing when I'd see her again. I went on a trip to do something nice for myself, but, like the rest of the world, I faced an unprecedented situation. My heart dropped to my stomach when I realized I had my mom's empty house to go back to.

CHAPTER 11

PRIORITIZE YOURSELF

———

Returning home was hard. I landed at LAX and my sister, Arelly, picked me up. Even though I was grateful I had someone to meet me at the airport, I still missed my mom. Often when I arrived home after long trips, she and Arelly would come into the airport and wait for me with a "Welcome Home" sign. I would run toward them with a smile and would wrap them into a big hug. However, this time was different. There was a threat of an international virus that limited travel and made everyone in the airport extremely anxious and afraid of touching. All I needed was a hug, but COVID-19 prevented physical touch.

I was excited to move forward through my grief by doing the things my mom loved: learn, travel, and meet new people, but the world was against me. I planned to go back to school in Washington, DC after my trip to Bosnia; however, three days after I arrived in Bosnia, Georgetown University announced that students should stay at their permanent addresses because the university wasn't sure how they planned to address the spread of the virus. I was so desperate to go back to school. I needed some constants in my life.

I mostly needed to see and hug my friends from whom I needed immediate comfort.

In the second week of March 2020, Georgetown announced that the rest of the semester would be virtual. The blue screen reflected off of my glasses as I looked in shock at the announcement.

Not only had my mom just died, but now I wouldn't be able to return to Georgetown or see my best friends for the rest of the semester. I inhaled and exhaled, but the knot in my throat wouldn't go away. I thought about all the plans my friends and I had. All the kind people who told me upon my return to DC that they would be there to nurture and take care of me. But now I found myself in Los Angeles, alone in my mom's house. What a different circumstance from what I imagined only a week earlier. I was sad and alone. All I wanted was to sit on the couch in my apartment in DC with my best friends and just talk or watch a stupid romantic comedy.

Arelly stepped up and offered to move in. I naturally said yes because having another person in my home made me feel less alone.

As the updates came in, we learned that the virus spread from Wuhan, China, to the rest of the world. We were living in a global pandemic from the likes we have never seen before. Not only was I still grieving the loss of my mom, but now we were living in a situation in which everyone had to remain socially distant.

Though I loved having someone with me in the house, I still missed my mom. I had never stayed in the house without her. I needed something to keep my mind occupied, so I bought several grief books.

I opened one of the books and flipped through the pages. I slowly took in the fact that I, a twenty-one-year-old girl, was reading grief books. I carried the book *Permission to Grieve* delicately to an orange hammock chair in the backyard. I crawled onto the lap of the hammock and leaned back, then closed my eyes. The way the hammock hugged me made me feel like my mom was hugging me. I pulled my feet off the ground and let the wind swing me. The wind pushed me as if my mom was rocking me gently. A calmness washed over me. Despite my mom's death and a global pandemic, I still had to finish my classes. After every online class, I would run to my hammock chair to feel a bit of love and comfort. I was so tired. I woke up, did classes, made food, did more classes, slept, then did it again. A few months ago, I was planning adventures with my friends, excited and hopeful for the future. Now, I found myself alone. I had no purpose. There was nothing in my immediate future that I actively looked forward to.

My friends called me to check in, and sometimes I was excited to talk to them, but sometimes I would grip the phone tightly in anger because I didn't want to talk to anyone. I've always been an optimist to the people in my life, but during this time I consistently took on a pessimistic view of the world. Friends would try to get me excited about things and I'd react with a sullen face. One of my best friends, Matthew, would always call with such enthusiasm. I wanted to meet him at his level and be excited with him, but deep down inside, I still felt empty. My dear friend Sania would Face-Time me every Sunday and we'd do face masks together—a little bit of self-care that was sorely needed. Nico and I talked most days because, like me, he lived alone, and we needed the company. Tommy and I connected once in a while and after every conversation, I always felt better. Whenever Rimsha called, we'd stay on the phone for hours talking about everything and nothing. My friend Maddie created a weekly virtual game night for our friend group, and that was something that helped me get through the loneliness I experienced.

. . .

The more I spoke with my friends, the more it felt like my old normal before my mom died. Then, I got a call from the executor of my mom's will reminding me to meet to go over taxes, investments, house repairs, and the rest. I was sucked back into my new normal. I tried this new normal the best I could, but I couldn't handle it. It wasn't that I couldn't handle it, it was more that I didn't want to. I missed being a child and throwing up my hands saying, "I don't know how to do it! Can you just do it for me?" However, I am my mom's only blood family, so her affairs were my affairs. I was lucky to have Susan, the executor of my mom's will and an old friend, help me through it all. I still felt overwhelmed.

One day, I was chatting with Maddie and an idea came to my head: "What if I come to visit you in Seattle? I just need to get out of this house and be with a friend." She considered my proposal, checked with her family, and called it a plan! Then, Margaret jumped in and offered for me to stay with her and my godfather Pat for as long as I wanted. A two-week visit turned into a two-month stay and it was exactly what I needed. While I was semi-okay at home, I wanted to fully let someone else care for me, and the best person for that job was Margaret. I loved living with my sister Arelly, but I wanted a parental figure to love on me. There's a reason she was my mom's best friend. Simply being around her made me feel calm. When she rubbed my arm or scratched my back, I was instantly ready to sleep, even at noon. Her home turned out to be a sanctuary place for me to be happy, sad, and all the combinations of emotions that came with it. My happy place, while staying with her and Pat, was the lake in front of her house.

Every single day after my virtual internship, I would go out on a paddleboard and navigate around the lake. I started on my knees feeling the slight waves of water caress my legs. Then I stood up and looked up at the sun kissing my head. I breathed deeply with each paddle and the calming waves filled my senses. Sometimes I would lay on my back for hours, letting the heat of the sun soak into me while my feet absorbed the cold lake water on the sides of the board. This time alone was special. Away from technology, and truly alone with nature, I could uncover all of my thoughts and feelings. One day, I looked up at the sky and yelled at my mom, "*Why would you leave me, mom?* This isn't fair! I can't do this without you." Other days I would cry softly. My favorite days were the sunny days when I felt closest to my mom. I looked at the clouds and swore she was watching over me.

Margaret's daughter, Megan, has two sweet girls that fill me with happiness every time I see them. I know my mom was like their adopted granny, and I could feel the connection they had with her in the way they chose to interact with me. One of my favorite moments during my stay was when I was sitting outside in a chair talking to my friends Matthew and Tommy. One of Megan's daughters calmly approached me and looked me in the eyes, but she said nothing.

"Hey, Girlie. Do you want to sit with me?" I asked. She simply nodded and snuggled into my lap. Feeling her soft curly hair nuzzled into my arm made me feel content in a way that I haven't been in a while. Then all of a sudden it started to rain, and Megan's daughter started giggling. We jumped up from our chair and ran toward the house. On our way, I noticed a brilliant rainbow. The kind of stunning colorful rainbow that pierces through a grey sky. Then she and I looked closer and saw a magnificent double rainbow. It was breathtaking. We stood there, hand in hand, as we studied the magnificent rainbow. Later, while Megan and I were paddle boarding, she commented that such a miraculous display in nature made her feel my mom's spirit was with us. Megan was like my mom's daughter before I was born. I loved hearing Megan tell stories about my mom.

The time I spent with my extended family was just what I needed. Being with my mom's best friend brought me comfort because I knew she was able to take care of me. I tend to naturally take care of others if I sense they are upset but staying with Margaret pushed me to let myself be cared for. My mom reminded me often to take care of myself first, but she often didn't follow that lesson herself because she always took care of others. One night, a sad song came on and my mind was thrown back to the day my mom died. Tears came gushing out of my eyes and without hesitation, Margaret brought me over to cuddle on the couch. She just held me without speaking and softly stroked my hair. That's what I miss most about my Mama: just having her hold me and rub my back, just having her near me.

Staying with Margaret and Pat was just what I needed; however, I had to go back home to Los Angeles to start the fall semester. It would be my first full semester living alone and being without my Mama. I was terrified.

CHAPTER 12

LOVE UNCONDITIONALLY

___

The hum of my professor speaking emerged from my laptop. My eyes were glazed over from video calls on Zoom. I loved my classes. They all focused on American education policy; however, I wasn't able to interact with my peers because of the virtual nature. I had to push a button to ask a question instead of raising my hand. One professor tried. She introduced fun activities to get us involved and connected, but becoming close with my peers made me wish I could be with them in the same room.

Living alone in my mom's home was a little spooky, and nightmares came to haunt me every so often. I thought of the toolkit my mom had left me and pondered how I could use those tools to improve my current circumstance that dragged on and on.

The first thing I did was buy myself a journal for reflecting called, "Let that shit go!" My mom would love not only that I was taking the time to reflect, but also that I found a journal with a smart-ass title. She found the most unique things hilarious. She had a dark and dry sort of humor that you couldn't help but appreciate. When she'd fall or a plan went wrong, she never took life too seriously. In those moments, and in everyone just like it, she found a reason to laugh.

Every day I woke up alone and had the choice of what to do with the day. One morning, I opened a cupboard and found the Mediterranean cookbook my mom bought for me a month before she died. I had been too busy with school and work to make any of the recipes, so I promised myself I'd take time to try as many recipes as I could. I held the cookbook to my chest. I carried it outside to my happy place: the orange hammock where I always feel my mom's presence. I looked through each page and placed a sticky note on each recipe that I wanted to try. It felt as if the book was a gift and a challenge from my Mama. I wanted to complete the recipes to show her I'm still following her guidance. I went to the grocery store to buy everything and was shocked that groceries for two weeks for only one person cost $200. On the second day of my Mediterranean cooking challenge, I made hummus using peanut butter, chickpeas, lemon, and salt. I invited Arelly over to devour my creation with me because, as mom would say, "Celebrate everything!"—even if you just made a bowl of hummus.

With a full stomach, I made my way back to my computer to face school and work. While both took a lot of time and energy, I loved my job. While my mom created our family including the Big Kids, Margaret, and many more, the family that I chose were my coworkers at the Beeck Center for Social Impact and Innovation at Georgetown. I started working for the center as a sophomore at Georgetown and fell in love with the community. I felt like I could be 100 percent myself and I always felt supported in everything I did. Also, they loved me for who I was and the effort I put into my work. Having an amazing mother is great, but also people held such high expectations of me because she was my mom. I felt pressured to be as selfless, as generous, as understanding, and as good at creating community as her. But my coworkers at the Beeck Center appreciate me because of who I am instead of who my mom is. I knew these coworkers were my chosen family a few weeks after my mom died. One day, Margaret brought in a large brown package from the porch. There wasn't a return address, and I wasn't expecting anything. I sat on the floor feeling sad and empty. She handed me the package and I smiled softly. I was just so tired, and it took so much energy to be excited about anything.

I took a pair of scissors and opened the mysterious package. I saw five colorful mini cards. I dug them out from the bottom of the box and laid them out on the table. I opened the tiny envelope and saw a handwritten card from one of my coworkers at the Beeck Center. A tear formed in my eye.

That is so sweet of her! I thought. Then I opened another card, and it was from another coworker. The tear fell down my face. Then I opened another card from another coworker, and another, and another until several tears slid down my cheeks. They also sent me some sweet gifts, but the cards meant the world to me. They didn't even know my mom. But they knew how much she meant to me and they cared so much about me that they sent the care package. This solidified in me that I was like my mom in that I am capable of creating community, and family, everywhere I go.

. . .

When I turned on my Zoom video, I was met with smiling faces from my coworkers at Beeck. Although I couldn't see them in person, talking to people familiar to me made me feel supported and less lonely. But then the call came to an end and I was alone in my house again.

It was Tuesday, my scheduled day to go grocery shopping, so I left my desk and made my way to the car. I turned up the music and passionately sang along. Music is something that always improves my mood. Once I finished my karaoke session in the car, I walked into the grocery store.

At the check-out counter, a young man started scanning my groceries. He wore a Hawaiian button-up shirt and was hunched over with his head looking down. My social nature came out and I asked him, "How's your day going?"

He paused from scanning and looked up at me for a moment. Although a mask covered half of my face, I tried to show kindness in my eyes. "Honestly, it hasn't been a great day, but I'll be okay. How are you?"

I was surprised by his honesty because usually strangers lie that they're okay when they're crumbling inside because they don't want to make others uncomfortable. I looked back at him and said, "Hah, I haven't had a great year. But I'll be okay." He laughed recognizing that the past seven months of the pandemic have made life hard on everyone. I appreciated his honesty and ability to not take things too seriously. It was refreshing to meet someone who admitted to the hard parts of life rather than always maintaining positivity. He finished packing my bags and looked up at me.

I picked up the heavy bags and said, "Well, I hope tomorrow is better" with a smile even though he couldn't see it through my face mask.

I climbed back into the car and bumped some cheery music because the interaction with the cashier made me feel better. I went home and grabbed the journal where I write letters to my mom.

"Hey, Mama!

Today was a tough day and I was just so tired, but then I met a nice guy at the grocery store who had morbid humor. Laughing about how shitty the year has been surprisingly lifted such a weight off my chest. I miss you. I miss your morbid jokes because they were the best. I remember how you always said that 'Life is too fucking short.' It's like you knew. I wish I had known. I would have been with you every day. But I know what you would say, 'Ya know I live alone, I'm fine. I know how to take care of myself.'"

I grinned. My stubborn mother. With the smile still on my face, my eyes started watering. I curled up in her bed and closed my eyes hoping she'd be next to me when I woke up.

. . .

The next Tuesday, I went to the grocery store. I made my way to the same cashier. He stood taller in his Hawaiian shirt uniform and picked up the groceries more enthusiastically. I made eye contact with him through the wall of plastic protecting us from each other. His eyes glistened a little in recognition. "Hello again! How's your day going?" The previously shy and timid guy seemed to be much more social today.

I grinned, "The year, overall, still isn't great but today is a good day. How was your week?"

"I'm glad to hear that. You should celebrate any day that doesn't suck. My week was fine, lots of work, but I got to enjoy the beach this weekend," He replied. He looked at me and occasionally looked down to continue bagging the groceries.

"Lucky! I love the beach, but I've been so busy with school to make time."

"You gotta make time for what makes you happy. Have you ever brought schoolwork to the beach?"

"Now that's an idea!" I replied with a smile.

He placed the last item into my bag and said, "Well, I hope you get to do something fun this week."

"I will!" I exclaimed as I took the bags from him.

Groceries in hand and a nice social exchange behind me, I was excited to carry on my day. I liked this guy's energy and appreciated in-person conversation compared to video calling my friends, so I decided to go back to the store the next day because I "needed" an extra banana. Sure, I could have waited a week, but I wanted to see if he worked on Wednesdays.

Sure enough, the mystery guy was there at 3:00 p.m. on a Wednesday and I approached him with one banana in hand.

He laughed, "Really? Just one banana?" He called me on my bullshit.

"Fine, should I go get a bunch?"

"Actually, yes, you should."

I left the register to grab a bunch of bananas and came back chuckling that my new friend had convinced me to buy five bananas instead of one.

"That will be $4, Miss," he said with a grin.

"You know what! You made me spend three extra dollars more than I intended to spend when I came into this store." I said with some lighthearted sass. "You should reimburse me or give me a $3 coupon for next time to make up for this, Mr.," I looked down at his name tag, "Will."

He laughed, "You're right. I will give you three free bananas next time you come, or $3 if I have it."

"Deal!" I replied.

I left the store smiling and carrying a bunch of bananas I did not need in my hand.

. . .

Later that day, Arelly came over to hang out, as she normally does. We sat together on the couch chatting away and I told her about my banana exchange. She just laughed and said, "You talk to so many people! I don't know how you do it." We started watching some random romantic comedy, and of course, five minutes in, the main character says, "I just miss mom so much." All of a sudden, me and Arelly's goofy energy went quiet, and the room got somber. You don't realize how many movies have dead parents until you lose yours. My eyes welled with tears and I tried blinking them away. I just reached out my hand and grabbed Arelly's. I didn't have to say anything; she knew what I was thinking.

A week later, I had run out of milk and all my fruit had gone bad. I arrived at the checkout counter with a smile on my face, concealed by my mask. His green eyes sparkled, "I see you bought more than four bananas this time! I'm impressed Ms.—?"

"Grace," I replied with a smile.

"Grace," he responded softly. He continued to scan each item with care. "I figured since I owe you $3 for making you buy extra bananas last time, I could buy you coffee? I finish my shift in an hour if you want to meet me next door?"

I blushed behind my mask. "Well, you do owe me $3!" I laughed. "Okay—I'll meet you there." I grabbed my bags and headed out.

I got home and faced my closet. *Is this a date? Is he just friendly? Should I put on makeup? Should I change my outfit?* I grabbed one shirt from my closet and inspected it closely. Nope! I tossed it on the bed. I held up a dress that was green and blue. *No, I don't want to look like I'm trying too hard.* I threw it on my bed. I grabbed another shirt and continued the process until I had twenty articles of clothing piled on my bed and I decided to leave with what I was already wearing after all that!

I walked over to the coffee shop a couple of minutes past 5:00 p.m., feeling a little nervous. I laced my fingers together and shifted my weight back and forth between my feet. Then he saw me. "Hey, Grace!" he said as he stood up. I shyly advanced toward him and took a seat. I kept both hands in my lap so I could twiddle my thumbs. I wasn't sure if this was a date, but it had been a while since a guy made me this nervous. "So . . . you come here often?" He chuckled at his terrible pick-up line.

I laughed along with him and the conversation just flowed. He understood my sarcasm and had this unique sense of humor. Then our coffees arrived, and he took off his mask slowly to reveal a trimmed beard and a sharp jawline. I didn't realize how handsome he was until I saw his entire face. He kept his eyes down, suddenly shy that he'd revealed himself fully. I took off my mask and smiled.

After this reveal, we recuperated our flow of conversation. Then I asked him, "Do you work full time at the grocery store or . . .?"

"No! Actually, it's just a second job I'm doing to get the money I need to pay for medical school."

"Oh!" I said with surprise in my voice, "Are you planning on becoming a doctor?"

"That's the goal. I swore I'd make my path, independent from my parents, but I might just end up doing the same thing that my mom does."

"What does your mom do?" I asked, noticing a twinge in my voice saying "mom."

"She's a nephrologist at Cedars. She treats patients with kidney issues."

I took a breath. "Oh! Wow." I held back from sharing more.

"Yeah! I have learned a lot about what she does, and it seems fascinating, but my dream is to be a pediatrician. I know it's not as sexy as nephrology, but I love kids."

I was still recovering from the sore subject. "Yeah . . . umm . . . uh." I stuttered. "My mom suffered from polycystic kidney disease, so the topic is very relevant to me. Her doctor, Dr. Kim, was just the best; my mom loved her so much . . ." I couldn't continue so I stopped speaking.

"I'm sorry to hear that your mom had to go through that. That must have been hard. Also, that's funny that your mom's doctor has the same name as my mom: Dr. Kim," he smiled softly. "But my mom goes by Dr. Jenny Kim."

I blinked hard. "My mom's doctor had the same name. Maybe it's a common name?"

"Was your mom in Cedars?"

"Yes."

I paused and took a deep breath. "Wow. Wait, so could . . . your mom . . . be my mom's kidney doctor?" My eyes filled with tears. I tried holding them back so that I didn't cry in front of a stranger. He reached out to touch my hand but remembered the rules of a pandemic. Instead, he gave me this look with his eyes that felt comforting — not pity, not confusion, just comfort. I took another breath.

"It could be," he said softly. "My mom told me about a patient she lost months ago, and she got pretty emotional about it. She told me . . ." he paused, "that she had a daughter."

I couldn't hold the tears back and a sob lurched out of me. The sound shocked me, and I covered my mouth with my hand, "I'm s-s-sorry."

"Don't apologize" he immediately responded. "I'm sorry for your loss. I can't imagine what you're going through. That must be so hard."

He gave me those eyes filled with comfort again and I sucked in my tears. Then I started laughing. A giggle first emerged, then a roar of laughter.

"What are the chances? Also," a chuckle interrupted my words, "and . . . I," I could barely hold it together. "I bawled on a first date . . . never done *that* before!" I continued to laugh, and then suddenly realized I had said "date" and instantly turned red. But he just looked back and smiled softly.

"Well, I can sure say this is the most unique first date I've ever been on!" He chuckled and allowed me to continue to laugh at the situation.

We connected immediately and continued to see each other most days after he got off work. Soon we upgraded from coffee dates to dinner dates to a trip to the zoo to me cooking for him at my place. I was happy. I had someone to hold hands with in public. It had been one month dating him and I was cuddled next to him in his bed. He was fast asleep. I looked at him and pondered how he could look so handsome even with his hair so tussled. Turns out he wasn't sleeping because, in the next second, he opened his eyes and jumped on me, saying ecstatically, "Are you watching me sleep? You, stalker!"

He tickled me and I laughed hysterically. Then he stopped and I looked into his green eyes. He concentrated on me and I melted. He smiled sweetly and leaned down to kiss me. Then I held him and cuddled him back into our sleeping position. As I felt his arms around me, an immense sadness washed over me.

All I wanted to do was call my mom in the morning and say, "I met this *great* guy." But she wasn't here to meet him or approve of him. This was my first real relationship, and my mom wasn't here to see it. She won't ever meet my boyfriend or any in the future. She won't be at my wedding to walk me down the aisle. She won't be there for me to call when I find out I'm pregnant. She won't be there to hold my hand when I give birth and she won't be there to hold my first child.

My mom was always there holding my life together and now that she was gone, I was the one who had to make all of my choices. I couldn't go to her for advice or go to her to tell me what I should or shouldn't do. I softly cried and buried my head in the pillow so my boyfriend, Will, wouldn't notice. He heard my sniffles and he squeezed me tighter.

But . . . I didn't want to. I didn't want to have anything good without her. What's the point if I can't bring my boyfriend home to meet my Mama?

"Shhh, shhh, shhh" He rubbed my back to calm me down. "It's okay. It's okay." He started.

I tensed up. "No," I sighed, "it's not okay." I broke free and grabbed my stuff and walked to the door.

Will sat up and crawled out of bed, coming toward me, "I'm sorry. You're right. It's not okay and it may never be. If you want to cry it out, do it. I'll just hold you, alright?"

I thought about explaining it, trying to tell him what I was thinking, but I couldn't. I was just so tired and sad. I nodded and he walked me back to bed. He held me tightly as I cried myself to sleep.

In the morning, I woke up and he was gone. I was too tired to be concerned so I just rolled over and softly fluttered my eyes open. As my senses awoke with me, I smelled something sweet. I pulled myself out of bed and found him standing in the dining room, setting the table. Then I turned my other senses on and heard James Taylor playing, my mom's favorite artist. I clutched his sweatshirt that I was wearing and walked toward him. "Morning, honey," he said as he hugged me and placed a kiss on my lips. Then a beeping noise sounded, and he reacted with a smile, "It's ready!"

He came back to the table carrying none other than the famous cinnamon monkey bread that my mom made every Christmas. Imagine the shock on my face. "You didn't," I said, happy and surprised.

"I did," he grinned.

"But how?"

"I may have phoned a friend. You know, Rimsha knows everything about you," he said with a sneaky smile on his face.

"*You* are the *best!*" I said leaning over to kiss him, but then I paused, "But . . . let's see if it tastes any good."

I left the table grinning and a tear welled up. I realized I didn't need my mom here to enjoy the good things. Sure, I'd miss her like hell every second, but I realized I can still tell her things. I ran to my room and wrote her a letter telling her all about Will.

. . .

Doesn't this seem perfect? Meeting a cute guy randomly at the grocery store? His mom being my mom's kidney doctor? Him being able to cook? Well, if you guessed it—none of it is *true*. I know you may not think this reversal is funny, but my mom would find it hilarious. She and I always made fun of books and movies that ended with the girl getting the guy, so I could never end my book that way, but I thought I'd try it out to see how it feels to be fulfilled by a boyfriend.

Although that relationship may be the picture-perfect movie ending, that is not my life. My life is perfect the way it is because I've found happiness and love in my family and friends. All I need is people to love and comfort me, and I've found that through my incredible friends and through my extended family. Love doesn't have to be romantic. Another value my mom exuded was unadulterated, unconditional love. She wouldn't hesitate to tell me what I did was wrong, but she'd always forgive me and treat me with compassion. I wasn't afraid of making mistakes because I knew it wouldn't make her love me less.

While I miss my mom every single day, I've learned that I don't need her physically with me to be okay. My mom remains with me through the people who love me.

CHAPTER 13

MAMA KNOWS BEST

Although my story doesn't end with a romantic finale, I have incredible friends and family that I am so grateful for. Amidst the chaos and sporadic sadness, I find moments of joy when I'm with the people I care most about. My sister Arelly was about to turn forty years old. That means the Big Kids would all be forty years old, at the same time, for one entire week. The big 4-0 and our mom wasn't around to celebrate it. Even though Mom wasn't here for Ale's or Arelly's fortieth birthday, we made it our own.

It was a tradition Mom started: When it was a Big Kid's birthday, the "person of honor" got to pick whichever restaurant they wanted to go to for their birthday. So Arelly chose a restaurant famous for their ribs. Given the pandemic, Ale, Arelly, Liz, and German arrived at my house, or "Mom's house," as we still call it, to celebrate, seven months after losing our mom. We thought about being sad and missing Mom, but I remembered the lesson she taught me: Celebrate everything. We sat around eating ribs and laughing and smiling. When it came time for gifts, I proudly handed Arelly a brightly colored birthday bag. "Here," I said excitedly. "Open it!"

She ripped the bag open and saw gray fabric inside. She pulled it out slowly and held it up and smiled, "It's so cute!" She studied it more and realized it was a customized gray sweatshirt that said "Arelly's 40th birthday mixtape" with a cassette player that had a Depeche Mode sticker on it, her favorite band. Liz made the design, and I ordered the sweatshirts. I gestured to German and Ale and Liz to open their bags, and they found identical sweatshirts. Everyone was so excited by the gift that we jumped up from our seats to dance and take pictures. There was so much hugging, joy, and happiness I almost forgot we were missing Mom. But of course, I couldn't forget; my Mama wouldn't let me forget.

Everyone went home, and I felt the loneliness creep in again. I remained in my mom's house living alone for three months. I loved my freedom and independence, but I missed my friends so much. It's funny. Although I grew up in Los Angeles, I don't have many friends here. Since I left for college, I have barely come back for more than three weeks in a year. I video-called my best friends every day, and although they made me happy, I just wanted to hug them. One day I was reflecting on my life with Susan, the executor of my mom's will and my mom's old friend. She said, "Grace. You should *not* be alone. You need to be with people. I know you miss your mom. You're doing too much at once; you need to take care of yourself. It's okay if you're mad at your mom for leaving you. It's okay."

All her words hit me at the core, and after she left, I called Rimsha, Nico, and Tommy and said, "I'm coming to visit you."

Joy filled my heart as I booked those plane tickets. I hadn't seen my favorite people since February, and I missed them so much.

Who cares about romantic fairy tales when you have the best friends in the world? This trip was my fairytale: I got to feel loved, hug the people I care most about, and laugh my ass off. I visited Rimsha in Louisville, Kentucky, for a week and got to meet her family for the first time, which was nerve-racking, but the nerves were unnecessary. On the night of her twenty-second birthday, her sister and I sang Rimsha happy birthday, then I handed her a small brown box. She looked at me with curious eyes that seemed to say, "What did you do?" She pulled off the ribbon and lifted the lid to find a birthday tiara and a sash that read "Birthday Queen!" She laughed loudly while saying, "OMG, you know I hate this stuff." Although she claimed to not like the cheesy birthday gifts, she wore that tiara for the next twenty-four hours. Being around her made me feel comfortable, calm, and loved. My favorite part of the trip was the naps we'd take together or when she would nap on one end of the couch and I'd do work on my computer on the other end. I had the best time. The next stop was upstate New York where I saw two of my best friends: Nico and Tommy.

Tommy picked me up from the airport, and just being with him again made me happy. He's the funniest person in the world. He dropped me off at Nico's house and I spent several days with him. One night, Nico decided to make ratatouille. And it was incredible. The perk of having an Italian best friend is that they know how to cook well. We ate with each other and watched a cartoon on TV; I was just so happy to be in the same room with my friend. It filled me with peace.

Lastly, I went to stay with Tommy, and it was such a fun visit. I've been sullener since my mom died, and while I can still laugh, it doesn't come as easily. However, being with Tommy, I laughed nonstop, and I truly believe that laughter heals many things; it can't heal loss completely, but it can bring warmth. He let me talk about my mom, complain about her, tell funny stories about her, and even cry about her. But the best day was when Tommy and I drove almost two hours to meet up with my dear friend, Matthew. The three of us together made me forget what a shitty year it had been. It made me forget the grief that losing my mom left on me.

It was such a fun-filled, happiness-inducing trip. But the moment I stepped inside my house in Los Angeles, alone, I missed my mom all over again. I've learned that the sadness will never subside. Often, my happiness is juxtaposed with sadness because when I'm having the most fun is when I want to recount those moments with my mom.

As a way of honoring her memory and to feel closer to her, I often reflect on the lessons I learned from her.

My Mama taught me so many things:

- As a child, my mom never hovered. She let me figure the world out on my own. If I fell, I'd learn to pick myself up again.
- She showed me reality. Every time we went shopping and were checking out, she would say, "Hey Grace, come here. Look how much you cost . . . come here." I'd look at her with eyes of guilt and offer to return some clothes to the racks, but she just said, "I'm not trying to make you feel guilty, I just want you to know what things cost."
- She taught me to be realistic even when I just wanted to be a dreamer. She'd say, "Grace! Stop pushing. If he likes you enough, he will make it happen. So just, stop pushing."
- As a consequence of her making me thrifty, I hated spending more than twenty dollars on anything. But in

response, she'd say, "Gracie girl, life is too fucking short. Just buy it. If you'll use it, buy it. If you won't, don't."

- I always wanted people to read my mind and give me what I wanted, but she told me, "You have to identify your own needs and advocate for them. You should always ask for help. What's the worst they will say? No? So, what? Move on."

- Forgiveness has been integral to my life for as long as I can remember, but that is definitely due to my mom. She'd tell me, "It takes too much energy to hate someone or hold a grudge. It's better to forgive them and move on. Just because you forgive someone doesn't mean that what they did is alright and that doesn't mean you have to be best friends again; it just means that you no longer hold the anger against them."

- She also taught me to be bold. Although she says I got my social skills from Papa, my grandpa, I think I got it from my Mama as well. She'd say the most outrageous things. They seemed outrageous because it was always the thing that everyone else was thinking but didn't have the guts to say. If someone said something hypocritical, she'd be the first to exclaim, "Really?" because she always called you out on your bullshit.

- From half-birthdays to the first time someone crushed back on me, to losing a tooth, or driving a car, my mom celebrated *everything*, and I do too. She and I constantly looked for reasons to celebrate as often as we could. She even celebrated my final exams season by sending me a huge box of snacks to share with friends. My mom was at every single birthday for her "niece," Rory, so when Rory turned seven this year—I was there. Birthdays mean a lot to the Rector Girls, and so do half-birthdays, because four celebrations are better than two.

- I learned from my mom how to express myself well, and concisely. During the international service trips for my mom's work, we had nightly reflections. I was always so eager to contribute that I would start word vomiting. To combat that, my mom developed a tactic. "Hey Gracie, every night at reflection time you can only share two times." I sat as a patient five-year-old listening to my Mama. "So . . . think about all the things you have to say and pick just the most important things that you want to share those two times." She even came up with a code word, "elephant" for when I was talking too much. Or she'd give me a nudge or kick under the table.

- My favorite lesson that she taught me was to never take life too seriously. It's something I strive for but it's hard to do. She could always find humor, even in the bad things. She would chuckle at inappropriate times or say something witty while everyone was crying and make everyone smile again. When I lost a student body election, I thought it was the end of the world, but to her, she'd say, "Gracie girl—it's just an election. Don't let it keep you down. You're only fourteen years old. You'll have a shot later."

- She may not have told me this, but what I learned by being my mom's daughter is that you cannot control life, but you can control how you react to it. I've always been a drama queen; whereas my mom had a calm soul that never panicked. Terrible things would happen to her. Plans would not work out the way she planned them. People let her down who she didn't expect to. However, she centered herself, took a deep breath, and focused on what she could control and what she could not. She could control the way she reacted and the way that she conducted herself, but she could not control other people or the flow of the universe.

I cannot bring back my Mama as much as I wish I could, but I can surround myself with the people I love in the meantime. I can cry when I miss her; I can smile when I remember something witty, she said.

After my mom died, I used to be jealous that others saw signs of my mom's presence and I didn't. I would yell at the sky and say, "Mama—why won't you give me a sign that you're with me, that you're watching over me?" However, in the last semester of my senior year at Georgetown, I was walking across campus to get to my building. As I journeyed along the brick road, a strong wind descended from the sky. The wind surrounded me tightly, causing my hair to float and my blouse to billow in the wind. The way that the breeze encircled me made me feel protected. The leaves danced in the wind and a smile spread across my face. With each step, the wind followed me. I realized that my Mama chose that moment, through the lively wind, to remind me that she is with me every step of my life.

APPENDIX

CHAPTER 8

"Pam Rector and Grace Rector." StoryCorps Archive. StoryCorps, January 6, 2020. https://archive.storycorps.org/interviews/pam-rector-and-grace-rector/.

ACKNOWLEDGMENTS

———

I want to first thank my Mama for giving me the strength to write a book about our life together. You're the reason I love writing. As a kid, you gave me notebooks and told me to write down what was in my heart. This led me to writing a mini book about a princess and a prince when I was six! Also, thank you for forcing me to write in a notebook on every trip we went on because that process made me better at discernment. You continue to be the motivation in everything I do, Mama.

I also want to acknowledge Donna, my late godmother, who made me believe I could achieve anything I wanted to. You were my greatest cheerleader and I know you'd be holding my hand through this experience if you could. I miss you and I love you so much, Donna.

Another person who has been a great source of support throughout this journey is my other godmother, Margaret. You are the most loving and affirming individual I know. Of all the tears I've cried throughout this year, the best moments were when I could cry and cuddle with you on the couch, remembering my Mama and your best friend. I love you so much.

The Big Kids were a big source of support for me during this endeavor. Through the beautiful stories you all told me and the excitement you had when I talked about the book—or the teasing (but what else are siblings for?). I love you Ale, Arelly, German, and George.

Rimsha Nazeer has been the shining star throughout a year of darkness. You are my person, and I thank God every day that He chose you to be my best friend. Thank you for sending me a card on my first Mother's Day without my mom, thank you for dancing with me to celebrate my twenty-first birthday, thank you for listening to me cry through the phone, thank you for getting mad for me when I don't have the energy, but most of all, thank you for loving me unconditionally and for showing that love every single day. I'm so lucky to be your best friend.

Thank you to Jacqueline Reineri Calamia and Ashley Lanuza for being such fantastic and supportive editors throughout my writing process. Your advice and expertise enabled me to publish a book that I'm proud of!

There are so many other individuals who have helped me get to where I am today, and for that I thank you.

My mom never said she was alone because she had her community to support her along the way. I've been blessed with a beautiful community of my own and I am grateful, especially to those individuals who believed in me throughout the journey of writing my first book. I want to thank each and every one of you for affirming me and for being my chosen family. Thank you, especially to:

Abigail Shipman
Adriana Ines Uy
Ajaya Francis Jonas
Alanna Granados
Alejandra Alarcon
Alejandra Ramirez
Alex Pappas
Alexandra B'Llamas Reynoso
Alice Arutiunian Wyman
Alondra Vega
Alyssa Perez
Amie B. Kosberg
Andria Wisler
Anita Velasquez Kinney
Anne-Marie Schaaf
Anthony Dato-on
Anthony Garrison-Engbrecht
April Gutierrez
Araceli Franco
Aracelia Fernandez
Arelly Saldana
Armando Franco
Barbara Busse
Bess Maisel
Bradley Zacuto
Brenda McMichael
Brenna Blaylock
Briana Maturi
Britta Engstrom
Brown-Sullivan Family
Carolina Chavez
Caroline Macou

Carolyn A. Espinoza
Cathy Rodriguez
Chris Haller
Christopher Murphy
Claire McKenzie
Conrado Arroyo
Consuelo Valdez
Cynthia Schneider
Danielle Oviedo
Darlene M. Fountaine
David Swarthout
Debbie Lynch
Debbie Morales
Deborah I. Dukelow
Demacont Ureted
Dominica Johnson
Donna Sorensen
Eileen McDermott
Elena Bove
Elizabeth Torres
Ellena Hyeji Joo
Ellie Hidalgo
Elmo Johnson
Elsy Arevalo
Emily Zenick
Eric Koester
Erick Alvarenga
Erika C. Derr
Erika Rodriguez
Erin Sauve
Eva A. Muñoz
Faber Monroy

Fiona Hellwarth

Francesca Piumetti

Franchesca Rybar

Gabrielle Villadolid

Gail Bromberg

Genoveva Villasenor

Geralyn and Rick Hornstra

German Manjarrez

Haazim Amirali

Harrison C. Nugent

Heather Rowland

Holly Hueston

Hudson Klass

Irma Cueva

Jacqueline Manzo

Jade Smith

Jamie Hazlitt

Jane Argento

Janette De La Concha

Janice Burrill

Jeanette Chavez

Jeanne Crawford

Jeanne DeWick

Jennifer DiPaolo

Jennifer Merritt

Jess Mulson

Jessica Evans

Jessica Flores

Joanne Nakawatase

Jordan Peterson

Josephine Graham

Joyce Gabbert

Juan Cueva

Juana Kawasaki

Judy Ferkel

Judy Windle

Julia Esqueda-Arteaga

Julia Kozlowski

Julia Phillips

Julianna Burlet

Justin Wang

Kaitlin Sheppard

Karen A. Bealer

Karen Guerero

Karen Maher

Karren L. Rector

Kate Barranco

Kathleen Bank

Kathleen Langdon

Katleen Saturné

Katy Buckner

Katya Acuña

Kierstin Duncan

Kristen Wong

Kristin Linden

Kyra Hanlon

LaShyra Nolen

Lauren Brown

Laurie Laird

Laurie Stewart

Liliana Bustos

Lilly Estrada

Lisa Jauregui

Liz Reinhardt

Lorena Alvarenga
Lorena Chavez
Lorianne Harrison-Reyes
LuLú Montoya
Madeleine Mousseau
Madison O'Hara
Maire Ford
Mando Mena
Marcos Gonzales
Margaret Lynch
Marianna Hernandez
Marilyn Augustyn
Marlene Wilson
Martha Prieto
Martha Robles
Mary Coletta
Mary Genino
Mary Lang
Mary Lou Chayes
Mary M. Ritchie
Mary Plumb
Mary Sanchez
Mary-Catherine Micka
Matthew Fisher
Maya Nyquist
Megan Choitz
Meghan Moore
Melinda Gass
Melissa Alvarenga
Melissa Nix
Melodie Rivers
Meredith M. Sweeney

Micaela Plummer
Michael Lynch
Miriam Arias
Miriam Crinion
Molly Ayers
Nancy Gallegos
Natalie Ward
Nathalie Danso
Nicole Bartels
Nicolo Andre Ferretti
Olsen Hanner
Pam Burrill
Paola Garcia
Patricia Coulombe
Patrick Furlong
Patti Martin
Phil Scholer
Phyllis Palmieri
Rachel Greenberg
Ray Shiu
Raymond Dennis
Rebecca Bostic
Rebecca Cunningham
Regina Rosenzweig
Rimsha Nazeer
Rob Lofaro
Roberto Calderon
Rosa Gonzalez
Sabrina Wesley Nero
Samantha Hartman
Sandra Ceballos
Sandy Hotz

Sania Ali

Sara Mijares

Saumya Shruti

Shane Martin

Sierra Hegle

Sonali Persaud

Stephen Murphy

Sue Do

Susan Leary

Susana Mendoza

Taylor Kahn-Perry

Ted Kroeber

Teresa Holden-Ilgunas

The Johnstone Family

Theresa Kiene

Thomas Scanlon

Thuy Tran

Tina Urrutia

Toni Rabinowitz

Tony Jenkins

Tracey Hom

Trish Garton

Trisha Burdick

Trixie Joy Aquino

Valory Banashek

Vandhana Ravi

Victoria Graf

Victoria Hamdi

Thank you to each reader for taking the time to listen to my story. I hope this inspires you to reflect on your life and continue the tradition of storytelling.